CRACKING THE CODE OF SUCCESS

HOW TO SET AND ACHIEVE YOUR BUSINESS, FINANCIAL AND PERSONAL GOALS!

GARY LANDREMAN

Bloomington, IN Milton Keynes, UK

AuthorHouse™
1663 Liberty Drive, Suite 200
Bloomington, IN 47403
www.authorhouse.com
Phone: 1-800-839-8640

AuthorHouse™ UK Ltd.
500 Avebury Boulevard
Central Milton Keynes, MK9 2BE
www.authorhouse.co.uk
Phone: 08001974150

First published by AuthorHouse 3/16/2007

ISBN: 978-1-4259-7948-5 (sc)

Library of Congress Control Number: 2007901874

Printed in the United States of America
Bloomington, Indiana

This book is printed on acid-free paper.

To Deborah
My Wife, My Love, My Partner

CONTENTS

INTRODUCTION

I'M SURE MANY of you have heard from friends, family, and fellow workers that "You should write a book." I, like I'm sure many of you have, said to myself that I would like to write a book, but for various reasons just never seemed to get around to it. Over the years, after many of my training sessions attendees wanted more. Their motivation was piqued after the class, and they wanted to read or listen to more motivating ideas. Well, the time has come for me to put my thoughts, ideas, and concepts into book form.

In order for you to understand my reason for writing this book on goal setting and achieving, I would like to take the opportunity in this introduction to lay out my background. There are many subjects that need to be discussed and learned in order to find success, but they all begin with knowing what goals you would like to achieve in life.

I have spent the last twenty-eight years in the selling profession. The greatest amount of that time I have worked in the food distribution sales business; I still do. The companies that I've worked for sold food and non-food items to restaurants, hospitals, nursing homes, schools, convenience stores, catering businesses, special events, and to any other business that purchases food and food-related items and in turn sells them to the public. This is a very competitive business and one that has changed significantly over the years. Due to consolidation, companies becoming "broadliners" (a company that handles all lines of products necessary for a food operation) and expanding nationally, the profit that was once enjoyed by the companies in food distribution and passed to the sales force in the form of commission has eroded. In this business, every broadliner carries pretty much the same product lines. As an example, we all sell Heinz ketchup. Heinz ketchup is Heinz ketchup, so as you can see, if you want to sell Heinz ketchup, which salesperson is going to get the business? The salesperson who sells the cheapest? Maybe. The salesperson with the strongest relationship? Maybe. The *professional* salesperson? Probably!

The problem in the food distribution sales business is that there are very few sales *professionals*. For many years, salespeople were hired right out of high school or college and were given very little training. They were told what their "sales plan" was, they were given the voluminous product catalog, and then when they failed to produce the desired sales and profit, sales management was amazed. The management in most cases didn't realize that they were a large part of the problem. They didn't see that a lack of a real training program, the poor middle management, and the poor way of selecting new salespeople were the main reasons most failed.

One good example of a poor hiring program was when the largest company in the food distribution business decided to give each applicant a personality and aptitude test to judge their probability of success. If the applicant "passed" the initial screening, he or she was then asked the same questions, although phrased differently, by three management personnel. The answers to these questions were studied, and a determination was made whether the applicant "passed." Of course this program failed miserably to achieve the desired results, and the company continued to have an exceedingly high rate of turnover in their sales staff. They continually passed up excellent salespeople because they were poor at test taking, and they hired book-smart people who couldn't sell. However, the management hid behind the successful test results and avoided assuming responsibility for the failure of the salespeople.

There has long been a standing opinion that the many successful salespeople in the food distribution business come from a background in some food-related field. For example, a chef may make a good food salesperson because he has product knowledge, an understanding of the sales process, and can be a consultant to his customers. Now there are some chefs who have made very good salespeople, but overall, most chefs are highly opinionated and have a hard time accepting other chefs' and cooks' abilities. So quite a few of them fail as salespeople.

The truth of the matter is that the background of the individual has very little or nothing to do with the success of the salesperson. The method I find that works best and leads to the lowest turnover rate is simply hiring by referral. By hiring a person referred to you by someone you respect and admire, you greatly reduce the risks associated in the hiring process. What matters most is the character of the person, the individual's desire and passion to become a professional and succeed, combined with the ability of the sales manager to bring out the strong points of the individual. Sales managers, because of the applicant's past failures, turn down many prospective salespeople.

Some sales managers do not trust their own ability or understand the situation the person may have encountered in previous employment. What management fails to realize is the importance of recognizing the applicant's strong points and then judging whether the applicant will respond favorably to the sales manager's direction. However, I must mention that there are very few good sales managers in the food distribution business. Usually a good salesperson gets promoted to a sales manager, and for the most part, they are given very little training. They fail because they expect every salesperson to sell the way they did, and when they can't, they get frustrated and leave.

The biggest difference between being a professional salesperson and a salesperson who struggles and eventually fails is planning. The most important facet of planning is goal setting. The plan and the goals must come from the individual. Sales management can have a plan in place for the salesperson, but the action plan to implement the work required to achieve the plan must come directly from the salesperson. Ownership of the goals and a complete understanding of the needed actions to achieve the plan are paramount if the goal is to be reached.

In life you never know when another person's life choices will have a profound and life-changing affect on yours. It happened to me very early in life; as a matter of fact, I was only five years old. My parents owned a restaurant, we lived in three rooms attached to the restaurant, and my mother was the person responsible for doing the food ordering for the restaurant. Each week she would inventory the refrigerators, freezers, and storage areas and prepare a list of products to order for the week.

I usually accompanied her on these tasks. As the week would go by, the salespeople would call on my mother, and she would order from various companies. One of these companies was called John Sexton Foods. Sexton handled a variety of products, but mostly can goods, and they were known for quality.

The salesperson for Sexton was John Winter. He was a distinguished-looking man, always dressed immaculately. He would enter the restaurant with a smile; He knew all the employees and would greet them by name. John was a very polite man, and even I—a measly five-year-old—he treated with respect.

The thing that stood out to me though was that John didn't just take the order from my mother, thank her, and leave like all the other salespeople did. John always had something new to sell. John would always have a sample, bring out point-of-sale material, or suggest to my mother that she try something new on her menu. John had a plan when he entered my parent's restaurant. John was a sales *professional*.

Years later I was very fortunate to join John in the food distribution business. For several years, we worked for rival companies, and he was always a good competitor. I emulated many of John's sales habits, and they served me well.

As I progressed in the business, it became quite clear to me that the salespeople who had goals and a plan to achieve them were the leaders in the field. I began to set goals and found that there was really no formula available to follow. When I spoke with the successful salespeople, they all seemed to have a different philosophy. So I began to research the subject of goal setting, and over the years

I developed curriculum and have taught goal setting and achieving seminars for many years.

I love the sales profession. Every day I am passionate about learning more about sales, and I have a passion for teaching what I have learned over the years. It's a wonderful feeling when one of my students relates a successful story of how he or she applied a concept learned in one of my seminars and it led to a sale, an account opening, a referral, or to a large commission check.

My goal in writing this book on setting goals and achieving them is to give to each reader, in plain simple language, a precise blueprint of why, how, and when to set goals and how to implement an action plan to really achieve them and to bring out your motivation to take action!

I hope you enjoy reading this book, and I look forward to your comments.

GL@GaryLandreman.com

CHAPTER ONE

WHY SET GOALS?

THE POWER OF the human mind is unlimited!

IN THE EARLY years of the Kennedy administration, President Kennedy set a goal to land a man on the moon before the end of 1969. Many people thought his vision was an impossible dream. However, President Kennedy believed in the power of goal setting and knew that his challenge to the American people was set in a solid realization that the power of the human mind is unlimited.

However, he knew that setting the goal was not enough. He knew how to motivate the American people and rally them around a national cause. He also knew it was necessary to set into motion an action plan to carry out the plan and a monitoring plan to gauge the success of the plan. As history shows, his goal was achieved. In July of 1969, man set foot on the moon.

A study at Harvard University between 1979 and 1989 measured the effects of goal setting. In 1979, 100 MBA students were asked if they had set goals for the future. Out of the 100 students, three had goals set in writing, thirteen had goals set in their minds, and eighty-four

ated that they had not set any goals. When
study was done in 1989, the thirteen who
their minds averaged twice the income of
r who had not set any goals; the three who
had written goals averaged ten times the incomes of those
without goals.

Goal setting, creating an action plan, and assessing
progress is a process. It is an everyday event that should
be the map of your life.

> **"SETTING A GOAL IS NOT THE MAIN THING.
> IT IS DECIDING HOW YOU WILL GO ABOUT
> ACHIEVING IT AND STAYING WITH THAT PLAN."**
> **—TOM LANDRY**

It is unfortunate that so many people get up in the
morning with very little purpose in life except to get
through the day. They lead for the most part a boring
existence just trying to make ends meet. I don't want you
to be one of those pathetic people. I want you to take full
advantage all of the wonderful things life has to offer by
taking control of your life. Goal setting and developing
an action plan to attain your goals will help you live a full,
rich, and productive life.

Unlocking the power of your mind is the key to
reaching your goals and setting you on your way on a
happy, tranquil, and rewarding journey. Understanding
the power of your mind and practicing techniques to
harness this power is a life-altering experience. You were
what you told yourself to be, you are what you are telling
yourself to be, and you will be what you tell yourself to
be. You and you alone have the power and control over

your life to decide what you are going to do with your life. You control how to live your life, what profession to work in, whom to spend it with, how much money you want to make, and how happy you want to be. You decide how much education you want, what type of relationships you desire, where you want to live, what to believe in, and only you can decide to unlock and unleash the power of your mind.

If you are a person who believes you are a "victim" of any circumstance or happening in their life over which they have no control, either put that thought aside while you are reading this book or quit reading this book. Nobody is a victim of anyone else; they are only victims of themselves. It is a fact of life that some people must overcome much larger obstacles than others must. Not all of us are dealt the same hand in life. It's how we perceive the situations we face and the choices we make in our lives that determine our emotional, financial and physical happiness. The world is full of countless examples of people who overcame serious obstacles that would have stopped many people in their tracks. Most likely you are not one of those people. You are probably fairly "normal." You have the normal problems of life. Perhaps you worry about money, a relationship, your employment, or your children's education. These aren't victim circumstances, these are normal, everyday challenges. But many people use these challenges as excuses for not attaining more in life. They hide behind "getting by" as the reason for not expanding their lot in life. The real reason is that they are lazy. They are satisfied with mediocrity. They are mired in the everyday living and, due to this reasoning, never unlock their minds. They are self-imprisoned in a web of never fulfilled dreams. Does this describe you? If it does, I hope you now realize that you can release yourself from the self-limiting beliefs that are holding you back from achieving your potential.

Your mind is the most powerful tool you will ever be able to use, and you carry with you from the time of your birth until the time your body dies. How well do you use this tool? Are you exercising and expanding your most important tool or are you too lazy? Do you believe you have enough education? Are you too busy watching TV and wasting your mind? If this describes you, quit reading this and take a job at the local gas station.

However, if you have the *passion* to become the best you can be, if you have the *passion* to make a better life for you and your family, if you have the *passion* in your soul to take control of your life and live your life the way you want to live it, if you have the in your heart to attain your goals and live your dreams, then read on. Learn how to make your dreams reality and how to turn your goals from mere thoughts and dreams into actions.

CHAPTER TWO

SETTING A FOUNDATION

DETERMINE YOUR VALUE SYSTEM

THE FIRST STEP in creating your goals is to determine your value system. Our values determine the way we perceive the world. Values are principles, and they are the foundation of our belief system. Values are the building blocks of character. All of us look at situations differently, and based on our value system, we decide if the action, opinion, or thought expressed is worthy of a response. Or perhaps it has very little or no affect on our family or us so we choose to ignore the situation. You must do a lot of soul-searching and determine what values are important to you. How do you decide what is valuable in your life? What type of people do you allow into your life?

Our values guide us through every day. Some believe that good health is important, so they choose to exercise and eat healthfully. To some people money has the most profound affect on their lives, so they work hard and climb their way up the corporate ladder. Others see their religion as the focal point of their life, and they dedicate their lives to helping those in need. Whether it's health, money, religion, education, happiness, travel, freedom, security, recognition, status, or any of many other values, you must determine which values are of importance to you and then build your goals solidly on the foundation of your values.

> "NO MAN CAN TELL WHETHER HE IS RICH OR
> POOR BY TURNING TO HIS LEDGER. IT IS THE
> HEART THAT MAKES A MAN RICH. HE IS RICH
> ACCORDING TO WHAT HE IS, NOT ACCORDING
> TO WHAT HE HAS."
> —HENRY WARD BEECHER

Your goals must be in congruence with your values. For example, if you truly don't care that much about money and creating wealth, you can't have a goal to be wealthy and live in an affluent neighborhood. If you don't have an overriding passion for your goal, you will never attain it.

So your first step is to sit quietly and write down what values you hold dear. What are your core beliefs? A core belief is a belief that never changes. It is a belief that is so important to you that you would never do anything to compromise it. It's a belief that you hold so dear that friends and family know where you stand on the issue and realize how important your belief is to you. You hold these beliefs so close to you and are so *passionate* regarding these beliefs that in any facet of life, you will not set aside your core beliefs to further your career or benefit your wallet. Your core beliefs make up your character and solidify your integrity.

ELIMINATE NEGATIVE INFLUENCES

ONE OF THE most destructive and devastating enemies of goal setting and achieving are self-defeating thoughts such as "I can't do it," "I'll never be successful," "I'll try, but I'm not sure I can do it." These thoughts will kill any chance for success and assure your failure. Never allow these thoughts to live in your mind. Fight all temptations to fall into that trap.

> **"OTHERS CAN STOP YOU TEMPORARILY—**
> **YOU ARE THE ONLY ONE WHO CAN DO IT**
> **PERMANENTLY."**
> **—ZIG ZIGLAR**

Remember: What you say to yourself you become. What you think of yourself you are. So negative thoughts, fears, and doubts must be exorcised from your mind. There is no need to be afraid of failing. Failure is only an opportunity to start again. Show me a person who never failed and I'll show you a person who never did anything. A certain amount of failure is needed if you are ever to be truly successful. One of the best ways to learn is from failure, because it teaches better than any other experience. When you learn from failing, you never forget the lesson. You control your life; you are the master of your fate. Do not allow negative emotions or thoughts to enter your thinking.

Can you imagine if some of the great people of history had listened to the negative people in their lives? What if Columbus had listened to the vast majority of the people of his time? Who knows when the New World would have been discovered? What if Henry Ford had quit after failing a few times? The automated assembly line and perhaps the industrial revolution would have been set back for years. What if President Reagan had listened to the naysayers of his time, those people who never had the foresight to see that the cold war could be won? If he had listened to those people, the Soviet Union and communism might still be in existence. These great people didn't let negative thoughts or negative people stop them from pursing success.

There will always be negative people in and out of your life, people who say "You will never be successful," "You can't do that." Jealous people love to be dream wreckers. Don't associate with negative people. Get them out of your life. If you associate with people with negative attitudes, they will only destroy your positive attitude. Don't waste your time trying to change them. They probably don't want to change. They are probably happy blaming everyone else for their miserable lives, rather that taking the blame and making the necessary changes to improve themselves. Just avoid them. If they are part of your family, be nice but keep your distance, and do not associate with them except when absolutely necessary; they will attempt to bring you down, and they will be a negative influence.

> "KEEP AWAY FROM PEOPLE WHO TRY TO BELITTLE YOUR AMBITIONS. SMALL PEOPLE ALWAYS DO THAT, BUT THE REALLY GREAT ONES MAKE YOU FEEL THAT YOU TOO, CAN BECOME GREAT."
> —MARK TWAIN

Don't get caught in the "victim" thinking. If you take complete responsibility for your life and the direction your life takes, you will never need to look for someone else to blame if you temporarily fail. You are the only person responsible for your actions. You and you alone are responsible for the choices you make. Once you realize this and take complete responsibility for all your actions and choices, you become very liberated and very careful to make choices and take actions that will lead to success.

Justification is a powerful negative emotion. We can always justify an act or a decision that is detrimental to another or ourselves by finding a reason that is not a fault of our own. When we do this, we make ourselves a victim.

Rationalization is another negative emotion that has no place in a positive person's mind. We can rationalize just about anything. For example, "My company never helps me so I missed my sales plan." If your company doesn't support you, change companies. Don't try to rationalize your failure.

All of these negative emotions fall under one large category heading—blame! Promise yourself, right now, never to blame anyone for your inability to succeed. Once you proclaim to yourself that you will never again blame someone else for your failures, you will have gained your psychological freedom, and you are now free to succeed.

Eliminating bad habits is an essential element in attaining your goals. Many of us get caught up in activities unassociated with our goals. Whether you're sleeping too late into the morning, staying up too late at night, or watching too much TV or some other useless way of spending your time, stop! In order to succeed you must have discipline. Analyze your habits and eliminate those are harmful to your success. Always ask yourself "What is the best use of my time, right now?" Then take action!

INCORPORATE POSITIVE
INFLUENCES

EQUALLY AS IMPORTANT as eliminating negative influences and negative thoughts is developing positive beliefs. Your beliefs are what determine your life's experience. Your success or failure is produced by what you have taught yourself to think. You must learn how to formulate positive thoughts and practice programming your mind with positive affirmations.

Self-talk is the most effective and powerful way to program positive thoughts into your mind. You are with yourself all day and night and talk to yourself continuously. Self-talk takes place at a rapid pace. Between 200 and 300 words per minute race through your mind. That's around 50,000 thoughts a day. If you learn to make these positive thoughts, you are programming your mind for success.

Unfortunately, people who fail are filling their minds with negative self-talk. They are saying to themselves, "I probably won't make the sale," "I never seem to win," or "I'll never make enough money to send my kids to college." With these types of negative thoughts racing through your head, there is very little doubt that you will fail. These are self-limiting beliefs operating in your mind, and they will lead to very predictable failure. But even worse is that once you fill your mind with these negative thoughts, it is very difficult to get them out. They become a part of your being, and many people never recognize how negative they have become.

Instead we must program positive thoughts into our brains. We must tell ourselves "I will make the sale," "I will win," or "I will make enough money to send my kids to college." Then we must go farther than that. We must practice the art of self-talk. We must train ourselves to be the master of our thoughts by sending in precise positive visions so we can receive positive outcomes.

All beliefs are learned and can be unlearned. Self-limiting beliefs must be unlearned by replacing them with positive ones. You can do this by practicing the following exercise, but keep in mind the positive thoughts you are placing in your mind must be real. In other words, you must have a passion for the beliefs you are transcribing into your brain. If you are not passionate about your beliefs, they will not become part of you. Beliefs are powerful.

> "ONE PERSON WITH A BELIEF IS EQUAL TO
> A FORCE OF NINETY-NINE WHO HAVE ONLY
> INTERESTS."
> —JOHN STUART MILL

Twice a day, every day, early in the morning and as one of the last things you do before you go to bed, do the following exercise. Have no more than three beliefs, convictions, or actions in mind that you want to become part of your life. The belief you want to incorporate into your life must be real, and you must be passionate about making it an important part of your life. The belief statement should be short, positive, and personal. Example:

"I will double my income in the next twelve months by doubling my sales." Next, sit in a quiet comfortable place, remain still, close your eyes, and completely relax for five minutes. To get into a very relaxed state, listen only to your breathing in and out. Try not to think of anything else but breathing in and out. After five minutes repeat the first belief you want programmed into your life twenty to thirty times. Don't count the exact number, just estimate. While you're repeating the belief, picture yourself being successful at the belief. Repeat the above exercise with the remaining beliefs. Each belief should be practiced at least forty straight days. If you do this, you will be amazed at the results. You will find your negative thoughts replaced by positive beliefs, and you will find the choices you make and the actions you take lead toward making the belief reality.

The use of this autosuggestion technique and the power of positive thinking are real and they do yield tremendous results. But you will only get the desired result if the process is followed properly. This takes work. It means dedicating yourself daily to a consistent routine that will lead to life-changing events. This is not a dream that suddenly comes true or a magic lamp and getting three wishes from some genie. This is a system that calls on your mind and the thoughts that you place into your mind to combine with your physical efforts to help you attain your goals.

> "YOUR ABILITY TO USE THE PRINCIPLE
> OF AUTOSUGGESTION WILL DEPEND,
> VERY LARGELY, UPON YOUR CAPACITY TO
> CONCENTRATE UPON A GIVEN DESIRE UNTIL
> THAT DESIRE BECOMES A BURNING OBSESSION."
> —NAPOLEON HILL

INCORPORATE POSITIVE PEOPLE INTO YOUR LIFE

SURROUNDING YOURSELF WITH positive people is a very important step to take if you wish to reach your goals. We talked earlier about the deleterious effects of negative people. Now let's discuss the salubrious effects positive, successful people and organizations can have on your life.

You have a choice in who shares your life. Pick wisely because you become very much like those with whom you associate.

When setting goals, many times you need other people to assist you in attaining them. Often you can work for and reach your goal by yourself, but you may need opinions or permission from other people. Take, for example, that you wish to attain a promotion or a different position in the company where you're currently employed. If you don't have a good relationship with the decision maker, don't bother making the promotion a goal because you're dependent on other people who may not hold your same thoughts or may be not as visionary as yourself.

It is true that positive people have a 60 percent better chance at succeeding than do negative people. Look around. Are you incorporating only positive people in your life? If so, great! If not, identify positive people in your organization and spend time with them. In the case of a work situation, you must deal with negative people who perhaps are not very good at what they do but they are in charge. Spend as little time with them as necessary and remain as positive as possible—or find a different job. Don't get hung up worrying about a promotion that you didn't get or a raise that didn't come through. In corporate situations, it's not always the most deserving employee who gets the promotion. Quite often, in fact, an employee who gains a promotion is not the best. They are often promoted because of personal preferences of the boss, or perhaps they are less controversial or less of a threat in taking the boss' job.

But above all, do not justify or try to rationalize that you are stuck around negative people. You must search for positive, successful people, and then incorporate them into your life. In order to be successful, you must have positive people in business, family, recreational activities, religious functions, and all other facets of your life.

Particularly in your employment, you must surround yourself in all directions with positive people. If you are involved in the corporate world and your leadership is negative, get out of that company. Hopefully your supervisor or leadership is a positive influence, and you should learn from them and develop a solid relationship with those individuals if you intend to aspire within the organization. But you should also search for colleagues and competitors who have shown themselves to be front-runners in your field and develop a network of successful people. In addition, if you are in a supervisory role, it is essential that you surround yourself with positive people and be a positive influence and leader. You never know where life may lead. You never know for sure how secure your employment may be, and having a positive leadership role within your company can help you attain your goals even if the place you achieve them may change.

Within every field of endeavor there are organizations and associations in which a person can become involved.

I encourage you to pick several and be an active member. Meeting positive people is often easier in these groups, because the membership is made up of people who want to be involved. These people are much more apt to be successful.

I can recommend a few of these organizations: Toastmasters International, the Knights of Columbus, the Moose Lodge, the Elk's Lodge, the Lion's Club, and the American Legion and the VFW if you're a veteran. There are many more, and you should investigate those in your profession. Ask successful people in all areas of business what organizations they belong to. Often they will sponsor you for membership into the group, giving you additional networking opportunities. If you have trouble finding an organization, check the Internet for those in your area, then contact the president of the association and ask to attend one of their meetings as a guest.

INSTITUTE GOOD HABITS

A HABIT IS a behavior pattern developed by frequent repetition. It becomes such a part of you that you do it without much forethought. You can change your old, ineffective habits and develop new, good ones.

> "OUR CHARACTER IS BASICALLY A
> COMPOSITE OF OUR HABITS. BECAUSE THEY
> ARE CONSISTENT, OFTEN UNCONSCIOUS
> PATTERNS, THEY CONSTANTLY, DAILY, EXPRESS
> OUR CHARACTER."
> —STEPHEN COVEY

In order to drop bad habits and institute good ones, you first must examine what you do and when you do it on a daily basis. Take an honest look at your life. Ask yourself some difficult questions. Be honest with yourself.

Life is made of time, and you can never recapture a moment once it's gone. Make a journal of your day. What time do you get up? Do you eat breakfast? Do you exercise? Are you organized in the morning? Do you have set appointments? Are you seeing your first client the same time each day? Do you read daily? Do you write daily? Do you have an organized plan for each day? What do you do if you have an appointment and have to wait for someone because they are not on time?

Let's talk about sleep for a few moments. The average person needs eight hours of sleep per night. So if you're to bed at 10:00 P.M., you should rise no later than 6:00 A.M. Do you tend to sleep longer? Do you want to change? Then discipline yourself to be in bed by 9:45 P.M., and do this religiously for forty nights. By this time it will probably become a habit. A person usually needs to repeat something at least thirty-five to forty times for the behavior to become a habit.

Take a good accounting of your health. If you are going to reach your goals, you must be mentally and physically in sound shape. Your mind is much sharper if your body is in shape.

If you're not exercising, start a program. When you begin an exercise regimen, it is important to keep it easy. As an example, if you decide to do sit-ups, do only twenty at first and work up progressively. If you choose to run, run a half-mile or so for the first few weeks and gradually increase the distance. A person tends to give up much faster if they try doing too much too fast. Don't burn yourself out and end up quitting the program by pushing too quickly at the beginning.

Have you read lately? It is very important to keep up on all aspects of your business and to become an expert in your field. Reading is a fundamental function of being an expert in your field. If your excuse is lack of time, get a book on CD or on your iPod and listen to it in your car. There is always enough time to educate yourself.

Do you write daily? Writing a short article or even a few notes about your business or a field you have passion for is a great way to bring out your creativity. Challenge yourself to write something each day. It's a great habit.

Of course, into your daily habits you should incorporate the previously discussed self-talk exercise that will help you visualize success and aid in achieving your goals.

"THE FIRST WEALTH IS HEALTH."
—RALPH WALDO EMERSON

APPLY DISCIPLINE INTO YOUR LIFE

SELF-DISCIPLINE AND PERSISTENCE are two traits that are common in all successful people. Setting goals, creating action plans to achieve them, and having the tenacity to persevere through the difficult times take discipline and persistence.

Persistence is self-discipline in action. It is applying, implementing, and sticking to the plan to attain your goal. Persistence is the single most important facet in the achievement of your goals. There are so many distractions and temptations thrown at us every day, that only unswerving persistence can save us from falling prey to procrastination.

> "LET ME TELL YOU THE SECRET THAT HAS
> LED ME TO MY GOAL: MY STRENGTH LIES
> SOLELY IN MY TENACITY."
> —LOUIS PASTEUR

The way to stay on target with your goals is to set a daily plan, in writing, with at least three actions you are going to take that day to reach your goal. By disciplining yourself to write a daily plan, you are preempting the natural tendency for inaction.

During the course of the day, at preset times, it is important to take a few moments to read your daily plan and make sure you are taking the actions you outlined in the morning. At the end of the day, record your progress, in writing. This will serve as a guide for the following day's plan.

The great thing about self-discipline is that very few people have it, so if you truly are self-disciplined you can quickly rise above your colleagues and competitors. There are too many people willing to go only the necessary distance in life. If they are upper management, they often expect their employees to go the extra mile, but rarely do themselves. That's exactly why they rise to a level and then leave the company. They do not expect of themselves what they require from their subordinates. As you rise in your company, don't fall into this trap. Expect more of yourself, do more than your employees, and life will reward your efforts.

> **"YOUR SUCCESS IN LIFE WILL BE DIRECTLY PROPORTIONATE TO WHAT YOU DO AFTER YOU DO WHAT YOU'RE EXPECTED TO DO."**
> **—RALPH WALDO EMERSON**

Having the courage and self-confidence to succeed is also important. Taking action at times takes courage. Not following the "normal" avenue sometimes requires tremendous self-confidence. Worrying about what other people may think regarding a novel approach often stops people from being creative. Have the courage to take a creative path when you believe it's the right course.

> **"IF YOU PUT OFF EVERYTHING 'TIL YOU'RE SURE OF IT, YOU'LL GET NOTHING DONE."**
> **—NORMAN VINCENT PEALE**

It is very important to get the facts of a situation correct and do all the due diligence required to assist in the success of your goals, but know when to take action. Overresearching and second-guessing are usually signs of a lack of self-confidence or insufficient courage to put your plan into action. More goals that are set and written are not attained because of inaction. Know when to pull the trigger, and be willing to take responsibility if your decision is not correct.

"By perseverance the snail reached the ark."
—Charles Haddon Spurgeon

The snail in the above quote took action. He wasn't fast, but he was persistent and followed his plan. It is much better to be slow than to be still.

CHAPTER THREE

SELF-ANALYSIS

WHO WERE YOU?

CHANGE HAPPENS. As we grow and mature, we change. We are not the same now as we were when we were thirteen. The way we look at the world, the way we socialize, the responsibilities we shoulder, among many more things change as we age. However, we can choose to be who we want to be, and we can choose how we react to any situation that faces us. The only difference between being torn apart by a situation and facing the situation with character is your attitude, and you can choose your attitude.

> "THE MOST USELESS ARE THOSE WHO NEVER CHANGE THROUGH THE YEARS."
> —JAMES BARRIE

Take a look back at your teenage days and even before. Think of how you felt about life. Think of how carefree you were and the joy you received out of doing the simple things in life. You got up in the morning, especially on a nice, beautiful, sun-filled day, with no more to do than quickly eat and run outside to see who else was out and you were off for the day. You played from morning until dark. Your life was easy and your heart filled with the wonderment of what it would be like when you were an adult. You didn't worry about growing up, because you felt like it were so far away that adulthood would never come. Think about all the things you did as an adolescent that knowing what you know now you would have never done. Think of all the fun times you had that would not be a part of your life if you, with today's knowledge, were too afraid to experience them.

As the years passed and you got your driver's license and then graduated from high school, life became a little more confusing. The opposite sex came into the picture somewhere along the road, and life really got confusing and a little more difficult. Then you had to decide what to do after high school. Do I go to college, do I take a job, do I sit out of school a year and then go back to school, or do I get married? All those decisions; it seemed so hard!

But what you need to think of is how did you feel? How did you become who you are today? What would you do differently if you could do it all over again? That life that you lived made you are who you are today. You need to know how you got where you are if you are going to develop goals for the future. You need to have a little childlike dreaming help you in the process. You have to remove the fear you have today and replace it with awe, an expectation of what can be. You must return to the childlike thinking that allowed you to be open to change and hopeful of great things.

**"PRETTY MUCH ALL THE HONEST TRUTH
TELLING THERE IS IN THE WORLD IS DONE BY
CHILDREN."
—OLIVER WENDELL HOLMES**

WHO ARE YOU?

BEFORE YOU CAN determine what goals you want to set, you need to know who you are today. From that happy carefree teenager, what have the years brought into your life? Are you still carefree, independent, and willing to take calculated risks? Do you still let yourself dream and follow your heart? Or have the years brought a more calm and conservative outlook on life? Have they clouded the once clear and exciting idyllic view of the world? Have you pigeonholed yourself into a dull and uneventful routine? Did you pursue an employment road that took you far away from the path you originally planned for yourself?

Whatever the case may be, whatever you have become, whatever road you traveled, you need to know who you are and where you are. What does your daily life consist of? Are you truly happy and satisfied with who you've become? Are you surrounded by family, friends, and colleagues who share your view of life and help you achieve your dreams? How is your health? Have you taken care of the gifts God has given you? Are you happy with the spiritual aspects of your life? Are you satisfied with your spouse? Are you happy with the paths your children are taking?

In other words, take an inventory of your life as it is currently. Be extremely honest, and write down everything that is taking place in your life. Document even the seemingly insignificant details such as your daily morning routine. Record what you do on a daily basis and what you don't do that you would like to do. This information will serve as a reference guide when you establish your goals. It will also give you a written document of your present life.

> **"The longest journey of any person is the journey inward."**
> **—Dag Hammerskjvld**

WHO DO YOU WANT TO BE?

The next step is into the future. Who do you want to be in the next phase of your life? Do you want to continue the current path that you just recorded? Are you content with the current course you have charted? Or is it time for a change? If you wrote down all the current things that are happening in your life and said to yourself "Where have the years gone?" or perhaps something like "I had always planned on saving much more money and retiring early, but I just never did." If these types of thoughts came to your mind, you're just normal. So many of us either wanted more out of life or thought they would attain more, but they didn't have a plan and they never took action. We were so busy making ends meet and taking care of the everyday tasks that we somewhere along the way lost track of our plans for the future.

How many people over the years have you heard say, "I really wish I would have done ..." you can fill in the remainder of the sentence with any of the many things that people wished they would have done in their life if only something had been different. It's really a shame that so many people never do what they want or become who they want to be and mostly because they think they can't.

So write down who you want to be in the future. Ask yourself "If I read about myself in ten years, what would I like it to say?" This takes time and does not necessarily need to be the goals you want to achieve, just who you want to be.

> "THROUGHOUT THE CENTURIES THERE WERE MEN WHO TOOK FIRST STEPS, DOWN NEW ROADS, ARMED WITH NOTHING BUT THEIR OWN VISION."
> —AYN RAND

CHAPTER FOUR

RISK ANALYSIS

Do you have the courage to be successful at whatever you want? This may sound ridiculous, but taking risk is not for everyone. Very little has been achieved without some level of risk. Of course we know America would have never have been discovered, the moon visited, or our freedom secured without heroes willing to take risks for the benefit of us all.

You must take an accounting of the risks you're willing to take to accomplish your goals. Some of this risk may be in terms of sacrifice. A yearned-for goal almost always takes sacrificing another want for the sake of attaining that goal. If you are going to achieve a goal, something else is going to be sacrificed. The sacrifice may be trivial, like not being able to watch TV or not being able to attend a sporting event, or it may be significant.

For example, your goal may be to double your income. In order to double your income, you must work longer hours, which will take away some of your time at home. You have to determine whether the goal of doubling your income, which of course will be very beneficial to your family in the long term, is worth spending less time at home. If you and your family are not willing to make that sacrifice, you cannot attain the goal of doubling your income. You have decided you are not going to take that risk. The goal isn't worth the sacrifice.

So before you begin to plan your goals, you must have the cooperation of all those who will either help you attain them or be affected by them. You cannot just undertake a plan to reach a goal without the needed cooperation or permission of those affected by your pursuit of the goal. Otherwise they will feel you have gone your own way and will not be a needed part of the goal achievement team, which is not fair to them or yourself. Or they will be dream wreckers and cause you to fall short of your goal or to abandon the goal all together. Either of these scenarios is wrong and unacceptable, so make sure you have the needed family members, friends, or colleagues behind you as you formulate your goals.

Are you ready to make a change in your life? Are you prepared to take the risks and make the sacrifices necessary to be highly successful? Unless you answer these questions positively, you are not ready to move ahead and make serious goals. Perhaps it's not the right time in your life to move forward and achieve the dreams you have always wanted. There is nothing wrong with admitting it's not the right time in your life to undertake new challenges and strive for success. Goal achieving is a process, and timing is vitally important. So if it's not the right time to pursue a certain goal, have the intelligence to set it on the side until the time is right.

But for those of you ready to move forward and willing to take some risk and make the sacrifices needed to be extremely successful, for those of you that are ready to fulfill your greatest dreams, there is a way in your heart, in your mind, and in the passion you need to make your dreams reality. The way is to set your goals, make a plan to achieve them, and then be passionate about following the process to make the goal a reality.

> "THERE ARE SOME PEOPLE WHO LIVE IN A
> DREAM WORLD, AND THERE ARE SOME WHO
> FACE REALITY; AND THEN THERE ARE THOSE
> WHO TURN ONE INTO THE OTHER."
> —DOUGLAS EVERETT

The best way to determine if you are ready to undertake the change necessary is to try to change small things in your life. If you are able to change the small routines that waste time, you may be ready to undertake larger tasks as time goes by. For example, if you believe you should go to bed earlier and get up earlier so you can accomplish more, set your sleep schedule as a habit to change.

Notice I referred to changing your sleep schedule as a "habit." Habits are sometimes hard to change. The key to establishing new habits that are good is to force through the first couple of months with good old fashion discipline.

> "WE ARE WHAT WE REPEATEDLY DO.
> EXCELLENCE THEN, IS NOT AN ACT, BUT A
> HABIT."
> —ARISTOTLE

From my experience, it takes doing something exactly the same way thirty-five to forty times for the action to become a habit. Over the years, I have tested this theory.

I have found that even taste is sometimes a habit. For over forty years I drank my coffee with cream and sugar. I decided this was an area of my life that needed change. There was very little sense in continuing to poison my body with sugar on a daily basis. I began to drink my coffee black with no sugar, and in about a month I began to enjoy the taste of the coffee in a black, sugarless, cream-free state. The first few days and weeks were troublesome, and I believe just the act of placing the cream and sugar into the coffee was programming my mind to accept the taste. When my mind realized that the cream and sugar were not going to reappear, my mind adjusted and I began to like my coffee black.

We are what we tell ourselves to be. We like what we tell ourselves to like. We do what we tell ourselves to do. We feel what we tell ourselves to feel. We are the result of who we are because we choose to be who we are.

We *choose* who we are! Freedom is in that statement! We have the freedom to choose who we are, what we want to be, who we want to associate with, how we want to react to situations in our lives, and the freedom to become a poor, fair, good, great, or excellent person!

Once we accept that we are responsible for ourselves and that outside influences are not to blame for our failures or our successes, we become liberated. We become free to incorporate changes into our lives that will lead to the outcome we choose. Once we assume all responsibility for our choices, we know every step we take will lead toward our goals.

The two most destructive forces in reaching goals are fear and blame: the fear to take total responsibility for failure; the fear to attempt a new ventures; the fear of what people are going to think; the fear of rejection by our peers; the fear of looking weird in the eyes of our family and friends.

These fears are always groundless. Dream wreckers in the form of family and friends are always in the picture. Often these people are jealous, and their fear of failure is thrust on you. They don't want you to try something new and be successful because of their lack of self-confidence. They don't want you to succeed, because it makes them feel like a failure. You need to either ignore these people or remove them from your life. You will not reach your goals if you let these people have influence in your life. They are cancerous and must either be removed or ignored. Ignoring them is very difficult, so my advice is to get them out of your life.

Look at failure as a chance to start again. There have never been any successful people who haven't failed along the way. Learn from your failures and move on. Just make sure you don't repeat the same mistakes, and you will be a better person by learning from your failures.

> "OUR GREATEST GLORY IS NOT IN NEVER
> FALLING, BUT IN RISING EVERY TIME WE
> FALL."
> —CONFUCIUS

Show me someone who hasn't failed and I'll show you either someone that has inherited money or a loser, and since most people don't inherit a lot of money, you've probably shown me a loser. Failure is a natural part of life that teaches us to keep trying. Those people who keep telling you that you can't be successful in a venture are most likely losers themselves. Get the courage to try something outside the "norm," make a plan, aim high, and *work harder than anyone else,* and you will have a great chance for tremendous success. If you're just sitting there hoping, wishing, and praying for success, the only thing you will get a is a sore rear end. Get off that rear end, realize that potential failure is part of the process, put the loser mentality out of your mind, and take action!

Blame is the other disease that kills dreams and renders goals useless. This has become an "it's someone else's fault" culture and a lazy person's society. How many times have you heard:

1. It's someone else's job.
2. I did my part.
3. It's the government's fault.
4. It's too hard.
5. I was only a half-hour late.
6. I'm tired.
7. I don't feel well.
8. That's not my department.
9. Can I go home?
10. Are we through yet?

You know people like this. They are always the first to quit and the first to ask for something. They never do anything without being asked, and then they expect to get the things they want. They always want something. They want nice clothes, they want a new car, they want to go out every night, they want money, they always want something except a job. These are the dregs of society, these are the useless citizens who expect to be taken care of by either family members or the government and then complain when they're out of money.

Blame is a dream slayer. Put blame out of your mind. Put blame to death, and don't allow people who blame outside influences for their failures into your life. There is no room for blame in your life. Once you realize that you have the power to live your life the way you want to live your life, you are liberated! You have tossed off the shackles of fear, you are no longer afraid of failure, and you blame no one. Now you are free to pursue your goals.

CHAPTER FIVE

LEADERSHIP

LEADERSHIP IS THE one trait that is essential if you are going to reach your goals. Even if you are a hermit alone on an island, you need the traits of a leader if you are to reach the goals you have set for yourself. The five traits I am about to describe are the key elements that need to be present in all walks of life, in every boardroom, and on every factory line if goals are to be met and success achieved.

There is no way a person can have long- term success if one of these elements is missing. Of course people who choose to be of poor character can make short-term gains, but none has ever achieved long-term success and personal satisfaction without all of these traits being a solid part of their character.

> "ONE MACHINE CAN DO THE WORK OF FIFTY
> ORDINARY MEN. NO MACHINE CAN DO THE
> WORK OF ONE EXTRAORDINARY MAN."
> —ELBERT HUBBARD

GARY LANDREMAN

1.VISION

THE TRAIT THAT distinguishes leaders from people who
just have great character is vision. Vision isn't just being
able to properly forecast trends in your business or being
able to guess correctly what your competition is going to
do. Quite frankly, these things are expected of managers.
Managers are a dime a dozen. If upper management
properly sets the direction and tone in the company, a
trained monkey can see trends and guess what direction
the competition is turning, keep sales increasing, and
profits coming in.

Vision is much more than this. Vision is understanding
not just how you're successful, but why you're successful.
Vision is an innate ability to see clearly the potential
success that can be achieved by following your plan and
being able to communicate your ideas clearly to your
team so that they can see and *feel* the same potential
result. They buy into your vision so deeply that it becomes
part of their soul. The people who follow you are so
convinced that your plan is right that they believe it is
their plan. Does this describe you? Do you have this type
of leadership ability? Probably not. Most managers don't
have leadership ability, and very few have the type of
vision I am describing.

Two great examples of vision in leaders occurred
in the last forty years. First there was President Jimmy
Carter. Although he was a very nice person of high moral
character, he nevertheless lacked the type of vision I am
describing. He tried to lead by telling the American people
how he felt we should live, how he felt we should conserve
energy, and how he felt we should save money. He never

communicated his vision clearly, the people never bought into his plan, and consequently it was his plan and not the American people's plan. The country became mired in some of the worst economic and least happy times of its history.

Then take the example of another President, Ronald Reagan. He restored the pride in America by having a clear vision of where he wanted to go, why he wanted to go there, how we were going to get there, and how the country would prosper once we got there. He clearly laid out his vision of lower taxes to spur the economy, to take on the Soviet Union and defeat them in the cold war, and to build up our armed forces to protect our citizens. He continually stayed on this message by going directly to the American people. He accomplished all of his goals, because the people believed it to be not just his goals but also their goals.

"THE GREAT SUCCESSFUL MEN OF THE WORLD HAVE USED THEIR IMAGINATION THEY THINK AHEAD AND CREATE THEIR MENTAL PICTURE IN ALL ITS DETAILS, FILLING IN HERE, ADDING A LITTLE THERE, ALTERING THIS A BIT AND THAT A BIT, BUT STEADILY BUILDING—STEADILY BUILDING."
—ROBERT COLLIER

So how do you develop this type of vision? Glad you asked. There are several steps you must take to employ this trait.

First, you must know yourself. You need to know intimately your strengths and weaknesses, and you need to know your profession inside and out. You must have confidence in your beliefs, and you must practice in life what you believe in your heart.

Second, you must have knowledge, complete knowledge of what you want to do, where you want to lead, why you want to get to that point, and a general way of how you're going to get there. You don't need to know exactly how you are going to accomplish your goal, because with every endeavor things change along the way and a great leader embraces change. A great leader recognizes that he doesn't have all the answers, and a great leader doesn't dwell on every detail.

Third, you must trust your team. You hired intelligent, self-starting employees, you taught them to be responsible, and you need to delegate responsibilities to these team members because success breeds future success. The real mark of a leader is how many of his team members go on to become successful leaders in their own right. Additionally, you must rely on your team for ideas and implement the good ones for the benefit of all.

Fourth, and most important, great leaders with vision give public credit to those team members who deserve credit. They are not afraid to give credit for accomplishments and take blame for failures if it benefits the team and advances the goal. Never forget to take all the blame and to give all the credit.

If you work hard at the above tasks, you will be successful more often than not in achieving your goals. Once you lead your team to success, they will follow you easier the next time. When your team begins to taste success, they will yearn for it, and they will expect to be successful. Once they expect success, it will come easier with bigger and grander goals. You can develop these traits. It takes hard work and time to develop vision, but I guarantee you will be grateful with the result.

> "VISION WITHOUT ACTION IS MERELY A
> DREAM. ACTION WITHOUT VISION JUST
> PASSES THE TIME. VISION WITH ACTION CAN
> CHANGE THE WORLD."
> —JOEL A. BARKER

2. INTEGRITY

INTEGRITY IS A firm adherence to core beliefs based on moral values. As a person and as a leader you must develop core beliefs. Core beliefs, as stated in a previous chapter, are principles and values that you will never violate under any circumstances. You hold these beliefs so close to you, and you are so *passionate* regarding them, that in any facet of life you will not set aside your core beliefs to further your career or benefit your wallet.

> "IN MATTERS OF STYLE, SWIM WITH THE
> CURRENT; IN MATTERS OF PRINCIPLE, STAND
> LIKE A ROCK."
> —THOMAS JEFFERSON

An example of a core belief is the freedom we enjoy in the United States. Our country was founded on the ability of Americans to be free: free from tyranny, free from foreign threats, free to raise our families in a safe society, free to become the best we can be, free to become educated and utilize our education to improve our position in life. Freedom is the cornerstone of our country and an unwavering core belief that many of our forefathers fought for and died protecting for future generations.

A core belief that you must possess to be a leader is honesty. A dishonest person is always a failure. They may have a short-term gain, but over time, a dishonest person always fails. Complete uncompromising honesty in all dealings is an essential trait in leadership.

3. DILIGENCE

DILIGENCE, AS DESCRIBED in the dictionary, is an earnest and persistent application to an undertaking. The word persistent is often used to describe a trait very important to leaders, and persistency is an important facet of leadership. However, the word diligence goes a step further. It is "an earnest and persistent application to an undertaking."

Diligence takes integrity and applies it to our work. It calls us to be stalwart in the pursuit of our goals. It requires us to have discipline and character in our desire for success. It necessitates us to base our work and to quantify our success on our value system. It strengthens our determination and fortifies our commitment.

> "IF YOUR DETERMINATION IS FIXED, I DO NOT COUNSEL YOU TO DESPAIR. FEW THINGS ARE IMPOSSIBLE TO DILIGENCE AND SKILL. GREAT WORKS ARE PERFORMED NOT BY STRENGTH, BUT PERSEVERANCE."
> —SAMUEL JOHNSON

4. RESILIENCY

RESILIENCY IS THE ability to bounce back: to bounce back from failure, from insecurity, from bad news, from a lapse of judgment, from rejection, from laziness, from a depressing occurrence in your life, from a missed opportunity, from poor health, from a goal you didn't achieve, from any happening that we as humans deem as a bad experience in our lives.

As humans we make mistakes and we fail. We sometimes hire people who we believe at the time have a good chance to succeed, but for one reason or another they fail to work out. Sometimes in our lives our motivation runs low or we suffer from ill health. We all have episodes in our lives in which we must call on our deepest resources to pull ourselves back to a point where we can excel.

As a leader you must be resilient. You will experience rejection, failure, and lapses of self-confidence on a daily basis. If you don't have these experiences, you're probably not working very hard. If you don't possess resiliency in abundance you will fail because you will stay down.

Each time you experience failure or rejection it is a great time to learn what not to do next time. If you work hard enough to fail and still stay in the business, you will eventually be a great success. The reason for your success is your resilient nature backed by your diligence based on your integrity.

5. INTELLIGENCE

INTELLIGENCE IN BUSINESS is the ability to look at situation and quickly and correctly decide what action to take that will benefit your business, prospect, or customer and move the prospect or customer in that direction.

Of the attributes it takes to be a leader, intelligence takes the longest to develop. This isn't because people aren't "book smart," but because very few are "people smart." The leader who is the most successful is the one who can develop the relationship with their team the quickest. Once they are able to have their team buy into their viewpoint, they have progressed from manager to leader. To do this, the leader must be an expert in their field, and that means a lot of hard work.

How do you become an expert? First, you must have passion for what you are doing. You must enjoy your work so much that you can't wait for the workweek to start. If you don't have this kind of passion in what you're presently doing, search for what you do have passion for and have the courage to make a change. Time passes too quickly, life is too short, and your profession occupies too many hours to be stuck in work you don't enjoy. Having a passion for your work adds meaning to your life, and when your team members see and feel your passion, they respond more favorably. Even your family will see and feel the passion, and it becomes contagious as your children try to emulate in their lives passion for their activities. I truly can't wait for Monday morning after a wonderful weekend, to awake early and have planned a week of building my business; it is exhilarating. To see that first customer of the week, or especially to make that first "cold call," is a tremendous experience. So figure out what you have a passion for and follow your dream.

> **"THE QUALITY OF A PERSON'S LIFE IS IN DIRECT PROPORTION TO THEIR COMMITMENT TO EXCELLENCE, REGARDLESS OF THEIR CHOSEN FIELD OF ENDEAVOR."**
> **—VINCE LOMBARDI**

Once you determine where your passion lies, you must be willing to make the sacrifices to become a leader in your profession. You must build your product knowledge, you must read and study techniques, you must work on your vocabulary and your listening skills, but above all, you must understand the keys to your business. For example, in my profession—sales—the only way to win in sales, the only way to be that salesperson who builds the relationship the quickest and gets the sale, is to understand and implement the key to sales. All professional salespeople know the key; they practice it every day. Those salespeople who you know are the best, those who make the most money, those who drive the nicest cars, those who win all the sales contests, those who customers always seem to want as their salesperson, all these people know the key to sales. This is so simple, yet so few salespeople, even if they know the key, use it. The key to sales? The only thing customers want is to know is how the product or service will *benefit them*!

If you're in sales now you know it! If you use the key, if you always use the key, you will have success beyond your wildest imagination. The problem with most salespeople is twofold. First of all, most salespeople are either too egotistical or too lazy to care or understand the customer's needs. Most salespeople only care what's in it for them. They want a sale, and sometimes they get a sale, but the professional salespeople of the world get the most sales because they truly care about the customer's needs, and they question and dig for the benefit the customer will receive from their offering.

In all professions there are keys the really successful people in the profession use and practice to be the best. What are the keys in your profession? What are the most important facets about your business? Whatever they are, practice them every moment you can. Become an expert in your field and help others attain success.

Let's go a step farther into the sales profession. I'm going to give you the key to finding what your customer wants. What they look for when they agree to listen to you. What benefit they want from your product or service. What their motivation is for buying your product or service. Your customer or prospect has only two motivational factors that will lead them to buy from you. Isn't that phenomenal! Salespeople are out there on the street day in and day out selling their hearts out, sometimes making a sale, most of the time facing rejection, and now you find out that if you only knew that there are a mere two reasons a customer buys, you would have made countless more sales? That may be a partially true statement, but just because there are only two doesn't mean you can recognize them. It doesn't mean that you can use them for success just because you know there are only two. It takes a lot of practice to understand and utilize the signals the customer gives you.

Money and/or happiness are the two reasons a customer or prospect chooses to listen to you or to purchase your offering. That's it. A customer either wants to increase their profits, save on their purchase, get rid of who they're currently buying from, make their employees' jobs easier, or some other reason that either makes or saves them money or improves the lives or the production of themselves or someone connected with their business.

Understanding that the essence of sales is the benefit your customer receives, and that your customer's buying motivation is either money or happiness, is a giant leap toward becoming successful in your profession.

However, now you must take action on this intelligence and use this knowledge to make sales. You are in the money-making business. Yes, it's true that you are genuinely interested in your customer's benefit from your product, but never forget that you got the job or started the business to make money. The money helps you take care of your family and allows you to live your life the way you choose. Knowing the keys to becoming a leader doesn't mean you'll become one. You must practice the techniques every day and with every team contact you have.

This step isn't easy; otherwise there would be a lot more leaders in the world. The fact of the matter is there are few leaders, because, as I said before, they are either too egotistical or too lazy to put in the work necessary to become a leader. How do you recognize poor leaders? It's really quite easy. They are the people who are always blaming someone else for their failures. They are constantly criticizing the company, but never offering solutions. They eventually leave the company and cause the same chaos at a competitor.

SUMMARY

The five traits of a leader:

1. Vision
2. Integrity
3. Resiliency
4. Diligence
5. Intelligence

PROBLEM SOLVING

LEADERS SOLVE PROBLEMS. Great leaders teach their team members to solve problems. It takes patience, understanding, and sometimes picking up the pieces, but great leaders realize the importance of teaching their fellow workers how to solve problems. Once the team learns to solve problems on its own, it raises the entire team to a new level. The result is that your customer gets treated better, gets serviced better, buys more, and makes everybody earn more money!

So you may ask, "How do you teach someone to solve problems?" It's actually quite simple. You teach them through example. If a problem arises with a customer, don't just handle it. Get one of your team members. Inform them of the problem. Ask for their opinion of how they would handle the situation. Tell them why they are right or wrong, and then have them involved in the problem-solving process. Make sure they are aware of all communication with the customer. When the problem has been solved, discuss with the employee the process that took place and why the customer is now satisfied. Impress on them—and make sure they understand—the importance of keeping the customer happy and the role that they play in the process. Explain to them precisely how far they can go to make the customer happy and what tools they have at their disposal to satisfy the customer. After a few of these training sessions, have the team member handle the actual problem with your guidance. Eventually you won't even hear of some of the problems, because you now have a team member equally capable of satisfying the customer as you are!

To do this takes a great leader, because the leader gives up some of their power. Only a person with self-confidence, courage, patience, and the ability to teach can delegate some of their authority and feel comfortable. If you're not one of these people, either you lack self-confidence, good communication skills, or you're not hiring the right people. You need people who can handle problems and satisfy the customer. If you don't have them, fire the ones you have and start over. If you do have them, teach them and your business will prosper.

By the way, you can use this same method in teaching your team members how to handle employee concerns. If you have middle-management people who have team members reporting to them, use this method to show them how to properly coach an employee who needs to get back on track. Have them coach their team members in the same manner you should be coaching those who report directly to you. One of the largest and avoidable expenses is employee turnover. Hire the right people, train them and then teach them how to hire and train. Never expect them to know who to hire or how to train. Teach them your methods and you will duplicate your success.

> **"Leaders are problem solvers by talent and temperament, and by choice."**
> **—Harlan Cleveland**

SELECTING THE RIGHT PEOPLE

Another role of a leader is to select the right people. No person has ever reached their goal by their work alone. You must have competent, trustworthy people working beside you if you are going to achieve your goals.

So you may ask, "How do I find competent trustworthy people to work beside me?" What I have found is that it is best if at all possible to work with people who are referred to you by someone you know and respect. This method, if possible, greatly increases the chance that the person you hire may work out because they were referred to you by someone who would not have referred them unless they thought it would be a good situation.

I In an interview there are very few things you need to look for. If the candidate has all the necessary credentials for the position, you need to determine the following.

1.   Is this someone you like?

2. Is this someone who seems to be of good character?
3. Is this someone who seems honest?
4. Is this someone who shares your interests?
5. Is this someone who seems intelligent?
6. Is this someone whom you would like to do business with?
7. Is this someone who you feel could handle failure?
8. Is this someone you trust?
9. Is this someone whom you would want to spend time with?
10. Is this someone whom you feel could take your place in the future?

You probably won't find anyone about whom you can honestly answer all these questions with a yes. But never hire someone who doesn't meet the first three questions with a resounding yes! This is a firm requirement. Additionally, only surround yourself in life with these types of people because life is way too short to be around people you don't like and are morally rotten.

> **"OUR CHARACTER IS WHAT WE DO WHEN WE THINK NO ONE IS LOOKING."**
> **—H. JACKSON BROWN JR.**

COURAGE

TO BE A leader takes courage: courage to believe in yourself, courage to believe in your goals, courage to stand up to criticism, courage to admit failure and above all the courage to stand solidly on your core values.

Belief in yourself is essential if you are to attain any goal you set. Self-reflection and honest self-evaluation are critical in order to develop goals and action plans that are real.

Belief in yourself is fundamental to achieving success: knowing that you are solid in your decision-making process, determined to carry out your plans, steadfast in your convictions and never second-guessing yourself because you thoroughly researched the subject or problem before making your decision, and you are confident that you have the correct solution.

The courage to attain your goals comes from your belief that the foundation of your goals are your values and that you have solidly built your value system so strong that the courage to stick with your plan to achieve your goals comes almost natural.

The courage to withstand the inevitable onslaught of criticism also comes from your solid belief in your core values. The dream wreckers come out in full force because they are jealous, envious, too lazy, or lack the self-confidence to challenge themselves to succeed. They have not built up the core value system that you have, and they are not strong enough to attain their goals. So they criticize those who are able and willing to make the sacrifices it takes to achieve goals. Usually these people are friends, relatives, or associates who want to bring you down to their level. They will do everything in their power to try to make you feel that you are foolish for thinking so big. They will denigrate you, and you may even lose some friends over your attempt to grow, but stay the course.

Because these people are losers, do yourself a favor and ignore them. Don't fight with them or try to win them over. If they are critical without understanding what you're trying to achieve and the system you are using to achieve your goals, you will never convince them. They are not worth your time. Forget them and stay on your goal-achieving course.

No one is successful in attaining every one of his or her goals. Although the system I outline will bring you a much greater chance of achieving your goals, you will still fail at times. It's what you do when you fail that counts. You must find out why you didn't reach your goal, go through the process again, restructure your approach, and implement the new plan. This is, of course, assuming that you still have the goal as one you want to attain and that your core values are in place.

You must think of failing to achieve your goal in the first attempt as a chance to start again. Analyze the process of your failure. Did you base your goal on your values? Did you write down your goal in detail? Did you write down your goal every day and review every night? Did you give yourself enough time to achieve the goal? Did you have the support of those you needed to achieve the goal? Are you willing to restructure the goal and try again?

Answering these questions takes courage, because the reason you didn't reach the goal was your fault. You are the reason you failed. You did something wrong. You need to admit your failure, fix the problem, and get on with the process of successfully achieving your goal. Taking the blame on your shoulders will help you in the next attempt. You do not want to face failure again, so you will take the necessary steps to achieve the goal and feel the exhilarating emotion of victory.

> "ALL OUR DREAMS CAN COME TRUE—IF WE
> HAVE THE COURAGE TO PURSUE THEM."
> —WALT DISNEY

CHAPTER SIX

SETTING YOUR GOALS

WHAT WOULD YOU DO?

WHAT WOULD YOU do if you could only win? Wow! What a thought. If you knew that anything you did, anything you attempted you could do it.

Think big! You can only win! Our first inclination is to be a little conservative when asked this question, but expand your world and include all of those things that you always thought were beyond possible: perhaps making a million dollars a year or ten million a year, taking a trip around the world. owning a very expensive car, buying a million-dollar home, living on an island (or better yet, buying an island!), paying for your children's college education. Whatever it may be. Whatever is a big dream of yours, dream it and then write it down in detail as though you already have achieved it. Make it so real to yourself that when you go to bed that night you think about what you wrote and perhaps dream about it.

This is called the C.O.W. theory, the Can Only Win theory. Release yourself from fear of failure, procrastination, and personal reasons that you have not accomplished what you've always wanted. If you open your mind to include those things that have always seemed a little or a lot impossible, you will find yourself realizing that you can achieve some of these seemingly impossible dreams. However, if you cannot envision it, and cannot imagine it, and do not have the passion for it, it will not come true.

Believe it or not, this theory is real and does work. If you try you win. Even if you don't achieve the goal you're attempting, you learn along the way positive things that will help you to attain future goals.

You need to utilize the C.O.W. method when you begin to formulate your goals. Force yourself to open up and reach into the innermost depths of your mind to pull out the dreams that have been smothered over the years by day-to-day life. Dare to bring those dreams out into the light of day, and don't be afraid to place them on the table when considering the goals that you are about to undertake. As a matter of fact, place everything on the table. Consider anything you can imagine. Wouldn't it be terrible to live out your life and retire only to say to yourself "I wish I would have tried that," and then realize it's too late?

WHAT WOULD YOU HAVE DONE?

WHAT WOULD YOU have done in your life if you knew then what you know now? Think back, be a Monday-morning quarterback and ask yourself what path would you have taken if the things you now know were available to you at that time. What direction would your life have gone if you knew then what you know now?

What would you have done, if you knew what you know now? Stop and think for a while. If you knew what you currently know now, would you have made the same decisions that you made? There is nothing wrong with making bad decisions; about 60 percent of all decisions are wrong. However, there is something wrong with knowing you made a bad decision and not correcting it.

Whatever is happening in your life, ask yourself these questions knowing what you now know. Would you live where you live? Would you work where you work? Would you have been better educated? Would you marry the same person? Would you have made that investment? Would you have saved more? Would you have hired that person? Would you be friends with your current friends? Would you bank where you bank? Would you be who you are? You can change things in your life if you choose and if you have the courage.

You only get one chance to live on earth, make sure you live the life you choose. If you find yourself in a situation that is untenable, have the courage to make a change. If not now, when?

So make a list of the things you would change now that you have more information. Using the knowledge that you currently possess, write down all of the things you would have done differently and would now like to change. When you're done writing, prioritize this list according to the most important to you and also the most practical to implement. As you proceed in the process of making your goal, things change and you will revisit this list often.

Many of the thoughts and dreams that you had when you were starting your adult life are still possible for you to accomplish today if you really have a passion for them. Those dreams that were put aside to take care of day-to-day activities are often the goals that people come to realize can still be achieved. Over the years, all of us became entangled in life's many unforeseen webs. Those years seemed to go so fast, and when they passed, it seemed we were off track and not realizing the gain and happiness we thought we would experience. But now is a different time in our lives. Now we can not only look back and learn from our past, but we can also look ahead and plan our future. We can take what we learn from this book and move forward in a precise step-by-step manner, accomplish our goals, and never have to say to ourselves, "Where did the time go?"

So what are these dreams for you? Do you want to finish your education? Do you dream of traveling? Do you want to learn to fly? Did you want a different career path back then? Do you want to double your income? Something got in your way and didn't allow these dreams to see the light of day, but now it is a different time in your life. You now know things that you didn't know then. Perhaps these dreams can now become reality, because you have some life experiences and can make these once impossible dreams possible.

> **"IT'S WHAT YOU LEARN AFTER YOU KNOW IT
> ALL THAT COUNTS."
> —JOHN WOODEN**

DECISION TIME

NOW IS THE time to begin to formulate your goals. Now is the time to start to make some decisions that will shape your future. Decision making is a process. You must lay the groundwork that will eventually lead to your goals. Based on the values that you have set for your life and the list of changes you would like to make, write down a list of goals you would like to achieve. The list should be long. You will pare down this list, so make sure to make this a complete and comprehensive list of potential goals. Make sure you have completed the steps above, and include in your goals some of the things you would like to accomplish if you could only win and some of the life changes you would have made if you knew then what you know now.

If you are like most people, you will probably have fifteen to twenty-five possible goals listed. When you're done writing, prioritize this list again according to the most important to you and also the most practical to implement. Take into consideration the cooperation that you will need from people in your life to attain your goal, and be honest when considering if they will truly be helpful in the quest to reach your goal. Quite often the people you think would help you most will never help you at all.

DEFINE YOUR GOALS

Now THAT YOU have constructed your list of potential goals, you need to begin to define your goals. The best way to start that process is to break them into categories. The categories vary with each person, but they can be something like business goals, family goals, health goals, investment goals, faith goals, and so on.

Now is also a good time to write down the possible problems that may arise when you try to attain your goals. Possibilities may include your boss is not in tune with your goal, your family needs to be behind you, you need additional education to meet your goal, and there are a multitude of other scenarios that could exist that you need to take into account. By making a list of the possible obstacles to attaining your goals, you can be proactive in either avoiding them or doing the necessary preparation work to advance your plan.

Now choose the goals you want to achieve first and the most realistic to attack at this time in your life. Taking into consideration the complexity of your goals, you will probably find it best to work on six to eight goals at one time. The list now should be broken down into short-term goals (less than six months), medium-term goals (six months to one year), and long-term goals (longer than one year).

Write a short paragraph about each goal.

EXAMPLE 1: GOAL = I WANT TO DOUBLE MY SALES.

Paragraph = I want to double my sales in the following twelve months. I am currently writing $20,000 per week in sales, and by this time next year I want to be selling $40,000 per week.

For right now this is all you need to write, but do this for each goal.

EXAMPLE 2: GOAL = I WANT TO LEARN TO FLY A PLANE.

Paragraph = I have always wanted to learn to fly, and I am going to get my pilot's license as soon as possible.

Doing this exercise expands the definition of the goal and prepares us for the following step.

PRIORITIZE YOUR GOALS

THE NEXT STEP is to prioritize your goals. This may not be as clear-cut as it sounds. Many times you may have a goal that is paramount to your family or career, but because you have not accomplished one of your other goals, you cannot start on the one you value most. An example of this would be that you have a goal to move into a new neighborhood and into a nicer home and a better school system for your children. However, you are not financially set for this goal because your other goal, doubling your sales and thus doubling your income, will lead to you being able to attain the new house. Sometimes you have to put off one highly desired goal until you achieve a goal that will be your foundation for the one you want most.

With that in mind, take some time to prioritize your goals. This may be the time to share your goals with your spouse or family. Having a support system is a powerful impetus to achieve your goals. Often your spouse or loved ones can recognize potential roadblocks that you don't see or aren't aware exist. By sharing your goals, you make them real outside the realm of your head. They are now in the mix of the real world, and a little pressure will come on you to be successful so you don't let down your family. Additionally, no one wants to fail, and sharing your goal increases the chance of success. Or at that time, they may share with you their own goals, and as a team you can take actions that will support and help each other reach your goals.

CREATE AN ACTION PLAN FOR EACH GOAL

Now YOU BEGIN writing in earnest. Begin by taking a goal and listing all the potential actions you could take to achieve the goal.

EXAMPLE 1: GOAL = DOUBLE MY SALES.

POTENTIAL ACTIONS = start earlier, see more customers, penetrate my current accounts, become a prime vendor to the account, collect faster, become more product knowledgeable in my profession, prospect better, ask for referrals, become a better listener, sell profitable categories, plan better, organize more efficiently, communicate better, use brokers, use specialists, get more customers to the company shows, use my time more efficiently, close faster, learn the facets of benefit selling, work longer, choose better customers, get my customers to order online, use flyer more effectively, develop better relationships, and so on.

Create a list of potential actions for each of your goals.

EXAMPLE 2: GOAL = LEARN TO FLY.

POTENTIAL ACTIONS = contact friends and family to see if they know anyone who teaches flying, contact the local airports, research online to become familiar with the requirements, check the library for information, call the FAA for referrals, look in the phone book for locations, and so on.

You can see by the above examples that some goals have many more potential actions than others. Make sure you take your time when doing this exercise, because these are the actions that will make up your plan to attain your goals. It's a good idea to begin the exercise, come up with as many action steps that you can think of, and then sleep on it and return the next day and continue. It is amazing how many times you thought you'd come up with every conceivable action and the next day you think of ten or twenty more. Our minds never stop thinking, even when we're sleeping.

After you have compiled a last of potential actions for each goal, write an outline for each goal. It can be a simple outline, but this is an important step, because you use it in the next phase of setting your goals.

OUTLINE EXAMPLE : GOAL = DOUBLE MY SALES.

1) Begin my day earlier & end later
   a. Get up at 5:30 A.M.
   b. Exercise
   c. Eat breakfast
   d. Leave the house by 7:00 A.M.
   e. See my first account by 7:30 A.M.—every day
   f. See my last account at 6:00 P.M.
2) Penetrate my current accounts
   a. Account ABC—get the paper business
   b. Account X—work on a prime vendor program
   c. Account Y—get the chemical business
   d. Account Z—collect faster
3) Prospect effectively
   a. Make a list of all the prospects in my territory
   b. Prioritize the prospect list
   c. Call on four new prospects per day
   d. Ask all of my present accounts for referrals
4) Utilize resources
   a. Formulate a plan to get my accounts to the company show
   b. Contact brokers to call on accounts

    c.Use in-house company specialists
    d.Get accounts using online ordering system
    e.Attend industry seminars

Once you develop the outline, use the points in the outline to write your action plan. Keep in mind that the goal is permanent until it is achieved, but the action plan is flexible because life is always changing.

ACTION PLAN EXAMPLE: GOAL = DOUBLE MY SALES.

MY GOAL IS to double my sales in the next twelve months. My plan to accomplish this goal is as follows.

Currently I am averaging $20,000 per week in sales. I have twenty-seven accounts. I average $740 a week per account. I plan on penetrating several of my accounts to bring my average account to $885 per week. I plan to open twenty-six new accounts during the twelve-month plan, so at the end of my twelve months, I will have fifty-five active accounts. These new accounts will average $685 per week in sales. This will bring me to an average of $41,705 per week by the end of my plan. I will do this by the end of twelve months.

I plan to start earlier in the day than I have been. My goal is to see my first account by 7:30 A.M. each day. If I don't have an account to call on at that time, I will be at a prospect at least having coffee and building a relationship with the management and staff. I plan stay out each day and see my last account or prospect at 6:00 P.M. or later. I plan to have more energy to do this by starting an exercise program and making sure I eat breakfast. I will do this by April 25.

My plan to penetrate my accounts is as follows. At Account ABC, I plan to get the paper business by identifying all of the products, using the available brokers, and asking for the business. I will do this by April 29.

At Account X, I plan to ask my supervisor to put together a prime vendor program because the potential is for over $6,000 per week, and we have a very good relationship with the owner. I will do this by May 20.

At Account Y, I plan to get the chemical business by sending the specialist in the account and showing the customer the benefits of our program. I will do this by May 13.

At Account Z, I plan to collect faster by getting an appointment with the owner and asking for more business, and showing him the benefits of paying faster. I will do this by April 29.

I plan to make prospecting the number-one priority. I will call on at least four new prospects each day. I will develop a list of all the prospects in my territory and faithfully each day update and prioritize the prospect list. I will do this during lunch each day. I plan to regularly ask all of my current accounts for referrals. I will develop a thank you card and send it to all my prospects at the appropriate time. I will do this by May 6.

I plan to get at least 60 percent of my accounts to the company shows. I plan to begin now to plant the seeds it requires to attain this goal. I will make a list of all my accounts and keep track of the various ways I use to get my accounts to the show, so I can monitor the results and use for the next show. I will do this by May 13.

I plan to go through each of my accounts and identify where I can use the help of brokers and in-house specialists and monitor on a weekly basis. I will do this by April 22.

I plan to make a list of the accounts that I believe could utilize our online ordering system, and I plan to present the benefits of the system to each of those accounts. I will do this by April 22.

I plan to research and attend at least one seminar every three months that will help me improve my performance and allow me to network with colleagues in my industry. I will do this by May 13.

As I am sure you can see, the above action plan is detailed. It will obviously be an evolving and flexible plan, but the goal is permanent. You need to write out each of your goals in a similar fashion. Some will be long and extremely detailed, and some will be just a few sentences, but either way they must be written. A goal like the one above can take up to a week or more to construct. It is vital that it is a realistic plan, but always push yourself a little. You will be amazed of the results once you begin this process.

"THIS ONE STEP—CHOOSING A GOAL AND
STICKING TO IT—CHANGES EVERYTHING."
—SCOTT REED

CHAPTER SEVEN

DEADLINES

DEADLINES CREATE MEASUREMENT

HOPEFULLY YOU NOTICED that every example of a goal in the previous chapter contained a deadline for completion in the action plan. The establishment of realistic deadlines for completing your goal gives you a measuring instrument. It helps create a sense of urgency and provides a time frame for the expected completion of the goal.

Without a deadline a goal is merely a dream. It would languish in perpetual limbo and would not be on your mind with proper importance placed on the successful achievement of the goal.

By placing deadlines on the goal and on the steps necessary to reach the goal, you can measure your progress and give yourself a timetable for completion. Deadlines track your progress and measure the reality of your expectations. So when writing your goal, make sure to set a deadline for each step of the goal and for the ultimate completion of the goal.

> "GOALS ARE DREAMS WE CONVERT TO PLANS
> AND TAKE ACTION TO FULFILL."
> —ZIG ZIGLAR

DEADLINES REINFORCE COMMITMENT

OBVIOUSLY, COMMITMENT TO the achievement of your goal is essential, and setting a deadline helps reinforce your commitment. *I am convinced that unswerving commitment to a goal is the single most powerful force to achieving the goal. A deadline is the lighthouse in the distance that keeps your journey toward goal achievement on the proper course.*

Commitment to your goal and to the completion of the necessary steps to accomplish your goal is fortified by the use of realistic deadlines. Many writers are only able to become productive when they are forced to be by a deadline placed on them by their publisher. The reason they are suddenly so much more productive and insightful is because they are forcing themselves to reach into their minds and draw out the thoughts that are already there. If a deadline was never imposed on them, the artistry in their brain would most likely never see the written page.

Well the same is true in the quest to reach your goals. If you don't place reasonable deadlines, your goals will never come true. They will simply be dreams that never meet reality.

> "THE ACHIEVEMENT OF YOUR GOAL IS
> ASSURED THE MOMENT YOU COMMIT
> YOURSELF TO IT."
> —MACK R. DOUGLAS

DEADLINES INTENSIFY
DEPENDABILITY

BEING DEPENDABLE IS a trait that is imperative to possess if you are to be successful in any profession, and being dependable to yourself is necessary to achieve your goals. Many times in our lives we forgo what is needed in our own life to aid a relative or friend. Although helping a friend is admirable, if the situation is not life threatening and could be done later, consider your needs and make sure your actions to help someone else are not detrimental to your dreams and aspirations. You have time frames to meet and deadlines to achieve, and doing things that don't fit your action plans will just delay your goal achievement.

Also, many times we get sidetracked and put our goals to the side to pursue things are not helping us reach our goals. Be dependable to yourself, and learn when to say no to activities that are outside of the goal acquiring actions. Learn to prioritize your activities and time to allow yourself to be dependable in reaching the deadlines you set.

> "WHEN WE HAVE BEGUN TO TAKE CHARGE
> OF OUR LIVES, TO OWN OURSELVES,
> THERE IS NO LONGER ANY NEED TO ASK
> PERMISSION OF SOMEONE."
> —GEORGE O'NEIL

DEADLINES STRENGTHEN DISCIPLINE

STICKING TO YOUR goal and the action plan to achieve it demands discipline. Deadlines strengthen your discipline by requiring that certain tasks are done by a certain time. They help keep you on track and solidify your resolve. How many people do you know who begin projects and are all excited about them, but the next time you see them they don't even mention that project again. They seemed to have so much passion and were elated about what they were going to do and how it was going to improve their life, and then ... nothing! They lack discipline and a precise plan, along with a proven method to achieve their goal that is based on their values. New Year's resolutions are great examples of a lack of a plan to reach a goal. People make the same resolutions year after year and think to themselves that this will be the year they stick with the resolution. "This year it's going to be different than last year," they confidentially say. No it's not! They haven't changed their heads. They are still looking at goal setting as a means to the end. Goal setting is an end in itself. It is a process that leads to an even better end by providing the vehicle to get there.If you asked those people who make New Year's resolutions what their deadline is for achieving their goal, I would bet that none of them has set a deadline. The resolution is merely a dream. They have probably made the same promise to themselves many years in a row and end up just fooling themselves into thinking that "This is the year!" No way! All they did was let themselves down again.

Most people have very little discipline. They think they have discipline, but they have never been tested. They stay within a comfortable surrounding, and they don't challenge themselves. Their comfort zone is really a hiding place, a place where they can retreat to give themselves a reason not to better themselves. A place where they can shelter themselves from expectations that they don't want placed on them. They live their lives within a small circumference, so they are protected by not wandering too far from what they know.

The lack of discipline and courage are the principal reasons so many people do not succeed. They live their lives in their perceived comfort zone and never reach their potential. When you have made your goals and attached a deadline to each step in the action plan, challenge yourself every day to dig deep into your character and be disciplined to complete each phase of your plan.

"THE QUALITY OF A PERSON'S LIFE IS IN DIRECT PROPORTION TO THEIR COMMITMENT TO EXCELLENCE, REGARDLESS OF THEIR CHOSEN FIELD OF ENDEAVOR."
—VINCENT LOMBARDI

CHAPTER EIGHT

CREATIVITY

BE THE BEST

IF YOU'RE GOING to do something, why not be the best? If you decide to do something, it's just as easy, and maybe even easier, to be the best at whatever you do rather than be average. It doesn't matter what you do, it's how well you do it. Whatever your profession, go to work each day determined to be the best and to learn each day something that will make you better tomorrow.

If you are a teacher, be the best. Make sure your students are prepared to do well on their tests and that they learn to become better people because they spent so much time with you. Put their real interests at the heart of your work and strive each day to make a difference in their lives. Be a role model for them by always being a solid person. Make it a goal of yours that one day at least some of your students will look back at the time they spent in your classroom as some of the most important days of their lives.

If you are a police officer, make sure you are the best. Take an interest in the community, be honest and trustworthy, and make sure that people who have contact with you go away with a positive image of the police force.

If you are a salesperson, be the best. Whether you are measured by sales, profit, new accounts, or increased commission dollars, make sure you lead the company. Work harder, longer, and smarter than all the other salespeople, and make sure that any customers who come in contact with you have a positive image of your product and your company. Then go farther than that. In every contact a with a customer, let them know that you appreciate them and their business. What will happen if you do this on a daily basis? Your customers will be more than customers; they will become your friends!

What is going to make you stand out above your peers? Creative thinking is very rare in most businesses and hardly ever utilized. Are you creative? Most people would shout out "Yes! I'm creative," when asked that question. Then when asked for the latest example of their creativity, they would be hard-pressed to name a single example. Most people do not use their creative powers because it takes thinking a little more, working a little harder, or sometimes taking a risk that may result in failure. It takes getting out of your comfort zone and opening yourself to risk. Most people do not think creatively on the chance they may be wrong or they may fail.

The extremely smart person is not always the most creative. In fact, I would suggest that in most cases, brains are not the most important factor in creativity. Hard work, determination, and a passion for success are more important than intelligence. Thomas Edison tested over

6,000 different materials before he found the carbon filament he used in his light bulb. Now that's hard work, determination, and a passion for success.

What will it take for you to become the best in your company? What qualities or abilities do the best people in your company possess that you don't? What will it take for you to acquire the necessary attributes to be the best? Are you willing to put in the necessary work to become the best? Are you willing to make the necessary sacrifices to become the best? Ask yourself these questions and answer them honestly. Then, if you decide to excel, begin to work tirelessly at becoming the best at what you do.

While you're working on becoming the best, start to think of creative ways to do your job better or to streamline the way things are done at your company. Compile a list of things that you think may make a positive difference for you or your company. It may be a way to increase sales or profit; an idea on how to collect from your customers faster; a way to improve service to your customers; a report that could more effectively show where improvement is needed. It could be anything small or large that is a creative way to make things better. Doing this will set you far above the norm. I assure you that very few, if any, of your fellow employees are coming up with creative ideas that will benefit your company or customer base.

By working on acquiring the talents that will make you the best in the company, and by constantly thinking of creative ways to improve, you will find yourself rising to the top in your field of endeavor.

"**THE THREE GREAT ESSENTIALS TO
ACHIEVING ANYTHING WORTHWHILE ARE:
FIRST, HARD WORK, SECOND, STICK-TO-IT-
IVENESS, AND THIRD, COMMON SENSE.**"
—**THOMAS EDISON**

THINK DIFFERENTLY

DO YOU GET caught up in the trap of thinking like everyone else? Do you hear complaints from your fellow workers and find it easier to "go along to get along" rather than think for yourself? Remember what we said in an earlier chapter about dream wreckers and how they can be so abusive. They rely on other people to be as miserable as they are. Stay away from those people. Let them destroy themselves, but don't get caught in their trap.

Creativity requires you to think differently. Be yourself and confident that you can rise to the top and attain your goals. The fact is that you can own that million-dollar house. You can put your children through the best colleges. You can become financially independent. And, yes, you can live your life the way you want to live it!

This is thinking differently, because so few of us truly believe that we can achieve anything we want. Let me repeat that, "You can achieve anything you want!" Some people may say that's just positive thinking, and they're right, but I prefer to call it thinking differently because it is different than the norm. Don't strive to be normal, strive to be exceptional.

In your business, only 2 percent rise to the top. They are not normal, they are exceptional. They think

CRACKING THE CODE OF SUCCESS

differently. Over the years they worked hard, acquired the skills needed to be the best, and were creative. They have set their pathway, and now it's up to you to blaze your own trail.

So while reading this, have you thought of ways to be different and creative? Has this thought gone through your head: "You know he's right, most of the people at work are just there to pass the time. They aren't coming up with ideas or better ways to do things"? OK, you thought that! Now what are you going to do? If some creative thoughts are going through your head, write some notes and as soon as you can, *take action!* And don't stop there. Continually challenge yourself to come up with newer and better ideas to implement in your work and at home. When you start this process, you will be amazed how fast others also begin to think creatively. They'll get out of their comfort zone and learn to take calculated risks because you led the way!

> "MAKE NO SMALL PLANS FOR THEY HAVE NO
> POWER TO STIR THE SOUL."
> —NICCOLO MACHIAVELLI

EXERCISE YOUR BRAIN

WHEN IS THE last time you read a book about your business or someone in your field? When is the last time you wrote an article about an element of your business? When is the last time you attended a conference that could help you in your business that you weren't required to attend? When was the last time you gave a talk to a group about your business? I bet there are not too many of you who have done many of these brain exercises lately, if ever.

You should be reading a book every week, or at least two books a month, that will help you achieve more in your business or that have the potential to improve your life. Nowadays there is no excuse not to read or listen to a book every week. That's right, I did say listen. How many hours per week do you spend in a car? Most of the time—if you're not on the cell phone—you are listening to the radio, wasting time when you could be listening to a book on CD, tape, or on an iPod. Now wouldn't that be a better use of your time? Of course it would!

Make it a habit (remember a habit takes doing it at least days in a row) to write something every day. It doesn't necessarily have to be about your business, but write every day. Begin by making some notes about things, events, or activities that you like. Then just start to write about one of the subjects until you have exhausted your thoughts on that topic. Come back to it a bit later and add more to the article or just organize it a bit better.

A good place to start may be to write a training seminar for your business or a training program for new hires. This is probably something you know a lot about and in which you have an interest. Or perhaps write about your life experiences. Whatever the subject may be, start writing every day and you will feel the creativity pour through your body. Once you start to write every day, it becomes addicting. Try it, it's great!

Attending meeting and conferences that relate to your business or an area that interests you cannot only help you learn and become more proficient in your work, but they are also great places to meet people and to network with others who have similar interests.

The Internet is an excellent place to search for opportunities and for groups and organizations that may be holding seminars or conferences in your locale. Sign up online to receive information about these conferences via e-mail and then *take action, attend and participate.*

Do you have "glossophobia"? I doubt that you do, but many people are afraid of public speaking. Speaking in front of people can be scary, but I will share with you the best way to overcome this anxiety.

By far the best way to temper the fear of speaking in public is to have a firm grasp on the subject you are presenting. Make sure that you have studied and researched until you have such a strong knowledge of the topic that your presence and demeanor denote strength, knowledge, and confidence.

Practice and rehearsals work well in helping you overcome fear and gain confidence. One method that works well for me is visualization, also called self-talk or autosuggestion. We touched on this in a previous chapter, but I will go through again as it relates to public speaking.

The method works like this. Let's say that you are going to present an hour-long speech to a group of about 100 at the local civic club. You have your talk composed, and you have practiced and rehearsed; you have confidence in your thorough knowledge of the subject matter. This is where visualization begins. Sit quietly, close your eyes, and start to visualize the entire speech. Begin with entering the building, thinking of the people that you will probably meet on the way in and all the possibilities that may occur. Get to the site early, check out the room, check your audio-visual equipment, decide from where you will enter, and think of all the potential actions you will need to take in order to have a "perfect" presentation.

Now visualize approaching the podium and beginning your talk. Run through the whole speech (not necessarily word for word, but at least the outline). Think of how you are going to use voice inflection, eye contact, gestures, and other vocal and physical methods to convey your thoughts. Think through any questions that your presentation may raise and the answers to those questions. Now you are coming to the end of your talk. Visualize the end of the presentation and how you will leave the podium. Repeat this visualization process at least five times and when you're on your way to the venue think it through again. By doing this exercise, your confidence level will soar.

Also, by detailing the speech in your mind and visualizing the exhilarating feeling that you will receive from giving a great presentation, you will tremendously increase your chances of giving a successful speech and greatly decrease the fear associated with public speaking because you have already been successful!

A great way to become proficient in public speaking is to join a chapter of Toastmasters International. There is a chapter of Toastmasters in almost every area of the country. Check the Internet for one near you.

> "KNOWING OTHERS IS INTELLIGENCE;
> KNOWING YOURSELF IS TRUE WISDOM.
> MASTERING OTHERS IS STRENGTH;
> MASTERING YOURSELF IS TRUE POWER."
> —LAO-TZU

DREAM

EVERYONE DREAMS. CREATIVE people add life to their dreams. What are your dreams? If dreams were real, what would your life resemble? When you're driving along and thinking about life and how things are going, what do you wish were different in your life? Do you wish you could travel more? Do you wish you had a different job? Do you wish you had financial independence? Do you wish you had more contact with your family or friends? Think long and hard. What do you dream about?

Now ask yourself the important question. What are you doing every day to make these dreams reality? What actions are you taking every day to make your dreams come true? Do you have the foundation set and your values in place so when you start to realize your dreams they can comfortably fit into your life?

You have the potential to make your dreams come true. You must, however, start to think differently. Creative thinking requires you to put aside all of the negative notions telling you that you can't do something. You have to begin to place into your mind only positive thoughts and ideas. Then you must take the necessary actions to make your dreams come true. Lock up the negative thoughts and unleash the positive actions that will lead you to the other side of the rainbow.

"ALL MEN OF ACTION ARE DREAMERS."
—JAMES G. HUNEKER

CHAPTER NINE

TAKING ACTION

SUCCESSFUL PEOPLE DO THINGS

WHAT DO YOU do when you get home? Sit down and watch TV? Well there is nothing wrong with relaxing and enjoying life, and if watching TV is part of your enjoyment, okay. But is it all the time? For many of you it is. You need to change. Truly successful people *do* things. They take the necessary actions to make positive differences in their lives. They don't sit and watch TV hour after hour. They plan, write, attend conferences, research, and network with people who can help them attain their goals. If you want to achieve a better lifestyle for you and your family, I can assure you it won't happen while you're watching TV. But it will happen if you put into motion goal-oriented action plans and take action every day on your plan.

W. Clement Stone said, "I think there is something, more important than believing: Action! The world is full of dreamers, there aren't enough who will move ahead and begin to take concrete steps to actualize their vision." Anyone can dream and brag about what they are going to do. How many people do you know actually took the actions necessary to realize their dreams?

Successful people are action-oriented people. They don't wait for their ship to come in; they buy the ship. You have to decide to be different that 99.9 percent of all people. That's right. Less than one-tenth of 1 percent of all people realize their ultimate dreams.

I'm sure you have heard the adage, "If you need something done, ask someone who is busy all the time." The reason you ask someone who is busy all the time is because they get things done! Do you get things done? Are you the one people come to when something important must be accomplished on time and with excellence?

One way to estimate if you are doing things that are leading you to achieve your goals is to ask yourself the following question, "Is what I'm doing right now the best use of my time?" Answer honestly, and you will find yourself achieving your goals quicker because you will be taking actions that will be conducive to reaching them.

Think about the most successful people you know. Or think of some of the most successful people in history. They all achieved their goals and dreams by taking action. They didn't stand by and wait for one of their relatives to die and inherit their money. They didn't wait for the government to give them a handout. They didn't wait to hit the lottery. They worked hard to achieve their goals, and they planned and took the needed actions to make their mark on history.

Let's look at a few of the famous goal setters:

Marco Polo had a dream of following his father's footsteps and going to the Orient. He took *action* on his dream and spent twenty-four years traveling and writing about his adventures in the Far East.

Christopher Columbus's goal was to find a new trade route. He didn't listen to some of the dream wreckers of his time who said the world was flat and that he would sail off the end of the earth. He took *action* and the world was changed.

The Founding Fathers of the United States had a dream of freedom and opportunity. They took *action* and put their lives on the line to achieve their dream. They defeated the largest and strongest army in the world to attain their goal.

Michael Jordan was cut from his high-school varsity basketball team during his sophomore year. He was very goal oriented and highly competitive with a relentless work ethic. He took *action*, practiced relentlessly, and went on to become perhaps the best basketball player in the history of the game.

President Ronald Reagan's goal was to win the cold war. Few people if any believed he could see his goal come true. But with the help of the Pope and the Prime Minister of Great Britain, they took *action*, and because of their *actions*, the iron curtain fell, the Soviet Union toppled, and cold war was won.

All of the above goals and dreams were big, and all of the dreamers took the necessary *actions* to attain their dreams. They didn't sit back and wait for destiny to knock on their door. They knocked down the door of destiny and walked through it.

"**Vacillating people seldom succeed.
Successful men and women are very
careful in reaching their decisions,
and very persistent and determined in
action thereafter.**"
—**L. G. Elliott**

PLANNING

Throughout this book we have discussed many facets of planning. However, because of the extreme importance of proper planning in goal setting, I feel we should once again touch on the subject.

Very little can be accomplished in life without planning. For those who say, "I prefer to wing it," I say that's probably because you're lazy, and I'm sure under further examination you're also probably failures. Can you imagine a professional ballplayer of any sport "winging it"? What would happen if a relief pitcher in baseball didn't take any warm-up pitches in the bullpen before coming in to pitch? He would walk most batters and hit the rest, plus hurt his arm. What if there wasn't a pre-season in football a time when the teams can practice their plays? Penalties and injuries would be more numerous than yards gained, because no one would know where to go or what to do. Well the same thing is true in business. Planning, practicing, warming up, whatever you call it, is absolutely necessary if you are going to be successful.

Planning and organizing your goals and the actions necessary to achieve them are activities that need practice and refinement over time to find the system that works best for you. However, the steps outlined in previous chapters and the steps that will be related in coming chapters are not optional if you are to attain your goals. There are no shortcuts!

Without proper planning and practicing the skills needed in your business, you are very apt to fail in the quest to reach your goals. Look at planning and trying to reach your goals as a trip. If your vacation plans called for you to drive from Maine to California, I have no doubt that the first thing you would do is reach for a map and try to ascertain the best way to get to California.

The same technique must be used to reach your goals. You need to find the proper "map" to find the best way to attain your goal. The difference is that you just can't buy the plan at the store the way you buy a road map. That is were a system of planning comes in. Learning how to research and discover the planning map is as important as the goal; without it you're traveling blind.

So understanding that successful people do things and taking action is the only way to get somewhere and attain success. Learn how to research, plan, organize, and prioritize properly, and you will be on your way to achieving your goals.

> "GOOD PLANS SHAPE GOOD DECISIONS.
> THAT'S WHY GOOD PLANNING HELPS TO
> MAKE ELUSIVE DREAMS COME TRUE."
> —LESTER R. BITTEL

DO SOMETHING OUT OF THE ORDINARY

Now I'm challenging you to be a little different. I want you to look for your own road and to use your creativity to reach your goals. Too many actions are taken because that's the way it's always been done. Is there anything worse than hearing that? If that was really the case, we would still be wearing loincloths and rubbing sticks together to make fire.

Break out of the normal, become exceptional, and blaze your own path. In everything you come across, question if the normal way is the best way? You will be surprised how many ideas you can come up with on how to do things more efficiently. Take a look at your home, your family, your business, your children's school, your bank, your investments, and every other facet of your life. I'm sure if you look thoroughly you will find a dozen or more things that can be done better, faster or more effectively. By just making a few of adjustments to your life, you will be in a much stronger position to attack your goals with passion. So from now on, look at everything and ask yourself "Is this the best way to do this?" If the answer is no, take action and change it!

Take a look back for a moment and realize some accomplishments that were made and how life was changed for the better because some people chose to believe they could make things better.

- Johannes Gutenberg invented the printing press in 1450 CE, and with the ability to print books, changed the world forever.

- Sir John Harington is credited for inventing the toilet in 1596, thank goodness!
- In 1752, Ben Franklin came up with the idea of the lightning rod, and because of that invention, saved thousands of buildings from fire.
- Thomas Edison was granted 1,093 patents in his lifetime. The electric lightbulb, the phonograph, and motion pictures were but a few of his achievements.

These creative people saw what was normal and decided to see if they could improve lives by doing something out of the ordinary. Now go back and take a look at your life. Can you improve on the normal? I'm not saying you should try to be like the extraordinary inventors listed above. I'm just suggesting that you may be able to improve on your everyday living by making adjustments in your life that will make achieving your goals and dreams easier.

> "THE MOST DAMAGING PHRASE IN THE LANGUAGE IS: 'IT'S ALWAYS BEEN DONE THAT WAY."
> —GRACE HOPPER

CHAPTER TEN

FOLLOW THROUGH

EDUCATION

THE ONLY WAY to have continued success in life is to continually increase your knowledge base. All of the self-help books, strategy books, or goal-setting books are only effective if the person getting the information has the knowledge foundation to take advantage of the ideas and the will and passion to implement the strategies.

To be a lifelong learner takes commitment: a commitment to yourself and a commitment to those you love. Never before has it been easier to be on the cutting edge of all aspects of information and knowledge. The resources that we have to stay informed are more various and sophisticated than at any time in history.

To name a few sources of information and knowledge: books, newspapers (they don't have to be local), magazines, Internet, Blackberry, TV (cable & satellite), TiVo, blogs, cell phones (text messaging), classes online, and so on. You can see there is a vast number of available ways to communicate and learn.

The question is whether you use these founts of knowledge as tools to help you reach your goal. Or are you using them as many people do, as toys?

Use these technological breakthroughs to help you attain your goals. Make it a priority to stay up on the new technology and learn how to use the advancements to your benefit. Carefully study the information you are allowing into your life and ask yourself, "What changes can I make to be better informed and more knowledgeable?" Then make the changes, stay properly informed, and continue the education process.

> **"WISDOM IS NOT A PRODUCT OF SCHOOLING**
> **BUT OF THE LIFELONG ATTEMPT TO ACQUIRE IT."**
> **—ALBERT EINSTEIN**

A PROMISE TO YOURSELF

IF YOU'RE LIKE most people, you have dedicated yourself to other people throughout your entire life. In your childhood, you wanted to please your parents. As you grew older, you dedicated yourself to friends or a spouse or partner. Later on you dedicated yourself and your time to your children, and so on through your life. Now it's time to make a promise to yourself!

I'm not for a moment suggesting that you ignore your family, friends, or any responsibilities. Just the opposite, I'm suggesting that you grow personally, so your family and friends will reap the benefits of an improved you.

Make a promise to yourself that you will follow through on the action plans that you have set to reach your goals. Make a promise to yourself that you will faithfully live up to the expectations that you have set for yourself. Make a promise to yourself that that you will honor your value system, stick to your core beliefs, and continue to learn and grow as a person.

You are the most important person in your life. Your personal growth in the areas of business, family, spirituality, intelligence, and emotional health are paramount if you are to lead a life that gives to others and to yourself. Make a promise to "pay" yourself first by striving to be the best you can be in these areas of life.

> "TWENTY YEARS FROM NOW YOU WILL BE
> MORE DISAPPOINTED BY THE THINGS YOU
> DIDN'T DO THAN BY THE ONES YOU DID DO.
> SO THROW OFF THE BOWLINES. SAIL AWAY
> FROM THE SAFE HARBOR. CATCH THE TRADE
> WINDS IN YOUR SAILS.
> EXPLORE. DREAM. DISCOVER."
> —MARK TWAIN

HABIT FORMING

SEVERAL TIMES THROUGHOUT this book I have brought up the importance of eliminating bad habits and forming habits that improve our lives and help us reach our goals. Forming the habit of excellent follow through in all areas of your life will vastly improve the chances of reaching your goals quickly and open up the possibility of living your life the way you want to live it.

As we discussed earlier, the process of forming a habit takes repetition. Doing something thirty-five to forty times the same way develops a habit. Most people must force themselves at first, but gradually the action becomes natural and part of their life.

Think about the people that you know who promise to do something but that never follow through. Doesn't it upset you when someone does that to you? It makes you avoid doing business with those types of people, because you can't trust them to get back to you. Well, don't be that type of person.

Dedicate yourself to excellent follow through. Force yourself to follow through by creating a daily checklist of projects that need your follow through. Refer to the checklist throughout the day, and monitor your progress. Before you go to sleep at night, make sure you have accomplished all of the follow-through tasks. If you have not finished them due to any reason at all, re-schedule them for follow through at a future date.

The creation of this follow-through list and the action of checking off the finished projects will help organize your life, hasten the progress toward achieving your goals, help you accomplish more in a shorter time frame, and give you a great reputation as a person that always follow through.

PERSISTENCE

HAVE YOU EVER met someone whose success you just can't understand? They don't have the skills, the intelligence, or the personality to be successful, but they are very successful. Some of these people are annoying. Some are downright rude and not pleasant to be around. Yet they are successful. Why are they successful? Most of the time it is because they are very persistent.

They may lack all of the other skills of success, but they employ the persistent skill to the max. They follow through, do the everyday tasks, and are always servicing their clients or calling on prospects. They make up for polish with tenacity and persistence. Often people end up buying from a person like that just to get rid of them.

Now I'm not saying that you should be the type of person who bugs people, but how persistent are you? Are you willing to make the sacrifices necessary to be highly successful? If you make the choice to be successful, you must work on your persistence. You will fail several times on your way to success, but will you learn from these failures? Will you be able to bounce back from these failures? Are you resilient?

You gain success through knowledge. You gain knowledge through experience. You gain experience through failure. In other words, the only way to success is through failure. That doesn't mean we try to fail; it means that failure is a natural component of success. The only way we couldn't fail is if we didn't do anything. When we take action, we sometimes fail. It's okay. Just make sure you learn from the mistake. Chalk it up as experience and move on toward cracking the success code.

> "PERSEVERANCE IS A GREAT ELEMENT OF
> SUCCESS. IF YOU KNOCK LONG ENOUGH AND
> LOUD ENOUGH AT THE GATE, YOU ARE SURE
> TO WAKE UP SOMEBODY."
> —HENRY WADSWORTH LONGFELLOW

USING YOUR TIME WISELY

TIME IS NATURE'S greatest force. Once it passes, we are unable to get it back. So what can we do to make sure we don't waste such a valuable gift? We can't manage time, we can only manage ourselves. We must create for ourselves a daily road map, a plan that will help us use our time wisely and maximize our efforts.

When seeking to crack the success code, you will have many and varied tasks to accomplish in a day. The preparation and planning that you do on a daily basis must always take into account tasks that are urgent and tasks that are important.

Unfortunately we spend too much of our valuable time responding to urgent tasks. These are events that are in our face, for example, a car accident or a family emergency. These are events that are urgent but do not add to achieving our goals.

Important tasks are defined as work that leads to reaching our goals. Important tasks lead to results and the reaching of our goals. Urgent task handling is necessary but rarely helps us in the attainment of our goals.

Each moment of the day you must ask yourself, "What is the most valuable use of my time, right now? What can I do to move along the process of attaining my goals?" Implementing the answer to those questions on a consistent basis will lead you to efficient use of your time and to accomplishing your goals faster.

"**Time is free, but it's priceles**
can't own it, but you can use
can't keep it, but you can spe
Once you've lost it you can nev
back."
—**Harvey Mackay**

REWRITING AND REVIEWING YOUR GOALS DAILY

Now WE GET to the part were we separate the few of you from the vast majority. This is the most important part of the book. Only a few of you will do the next required step that will crack the code of success for you. Because it takes a daily commitment and calls on you to be totally consistent, most of you will not do the following. But for those of you who will, I *guarantee that it will change your life* and lead to unbelievable success. Unless you do the following, every day, the time you have put into reading this book has been wasted.

Every morning before you begin your daily activities, sit down and either on your computer, in your daily planner, or on a piece of paper write down your goals. Do not refer to any list when doing this. Do it completely from memory. Write them as though you have already accomplished them, and put a deadline after them.

EXAMPLE: I MAKE 1 MILLION $ PER
YEARDEADLINE

EXAMPLE: I DOUBLED MY SALES
DEADLINE

EXAMPLE: I LEARNED HOW TO FLY
DEADLINE

THESE GOALS WILL already have an action plan established, and you will probably have five to seven goals that you are working on at one time. After you write each goal, write down at least one action that you will take that day to further along the progress toward achieving each goal.

Every evening before going to bed, read the goals you wrote down that morning and the actions attached to them. Ask yourself, "Am I farther along now toward achieving my goals than I was when I got up this morning?"

After a few months of doing this, you will find yourself in the habit of working toward your goals even when they are not at the top of your mind. You will also find that the order of your goals change with time. The way you write them often changes, and the deadlines even change with time. This is all okay. As long as you are making progress, you are going in the correct direction.

When you achieve one of your goals or find that due to circumstances or life changes that the goal is no longer feasible, replace it with another. Make sure the action plan is in place and that you have the cooperation of those that you will need to achieve the goal.

Now that wasn't so hard was it? No it's not, but still most of you will not do it *every day*! You're too lazy, or you start out doing it and since you don't see immediate results, lapse back into your comfort zone. Don't let that happen to you—stick with it and enjoy the life-changing events that will follow.

Now please go back and read the previous seven paragraphs again!

> "WHATEVER YOU VIVIDLY IMAGINE, ARDENTLY DESIRE, SINCERELY BELIEVE, AND ENTHUSIASTICALLY ACT UPON ... MUST INEVITABLY COME TO PASS!"
> —PAUL J. MEYER

FINAL NOTES

ARE YOU PASSIONATE ABOUT SUCCESS?

THINK OF THE most successful people in the last hundred years or so. What do they all have in common? Here are a few of the highly successful people I can think of, and I'm sure there are many more: Thomas Edison, Henry Ford, Albert Einstein, Babe Ruth, Ty Cobb, Franklin D. Roosevelt, Vince Lombardi, John F. Kennedy, Ronald Reagan, Margaret Thatcher, Mohammed Ali, Michael Jordan, Mother Teresa, Michael Eisner, Lee Iacocca, Donald Trump, Oprah Winfrey, Robert Allen, and Bob Hope. All were passionate about what they did in life and the success they enjoyed. They inspired the people around them to be better, and they excelled at their profession because they were passionate.

Although they all came from different backgrounds and had different careers and ideals, they all were passionate about being the best they could be at what they did.

Are you passionate enough to be highly successful? Do you have the drive and passion to be the best? Are you willing to make the sacrifices, go through the trials, and face the failures that you will experience on the way to success? When you talk to the people in your company, do they feel and comment on your passion?

What is passion and how do you attain it? Passion is that feeling in your heart that what you are doing and the way that you are doing it not only is right and good, but also inspires other people to become better at what they do. Passion is that feeling of overwhelming satisfaction that you have touched someone's life in a positive way and have succeeded in bringing up the level of excellence. Passion is enjoying what you are doing not because it brings in an income, but because it brings joy into your life and into the lives of all you touch. Passion is the feeling of accomplishment that comes with being the best at what you do and helping others reach that level with you.

You attain passion by being yourself and having core values and a belief structure that are based not only on bringing yourself up the ladder of success, but also helping others to reach a level they never thought possible. You attain passion by challenging yourself to always not just succeed at what you do, but to always strive for excellence in everything you do. You attain passion by never letting go of your core values, no matter the outcome, and by realizing that it's the people you help and touch in a positive manner along the way that leads to true success.

ARE YOU PASSIONATE ABOUT LIFE?

AS A FINAL note, cracking the code of success has only one goal: a better life for you, your family, and associates. Living your life the way you want to live it should be a goal for all of us. We are given a very precious gift, the gift of life, and we are given the power to choose how we want to spend the hours of our life. I hope that this book has helped even in a small way to kindle the fire that burns within each of us to grow into a burning passion to truly go forward and live our life the way we choose to live it.

We are also called on to pass the knowledge to those we know that will benefit from our success. By helping those in our business and family succeed, we become better for their improvement. We have found the combination to the code, and by passing that knowledge to others, we strengthen our own resolve to be better people. Our passion passed on to others creates a firestorm of success and allows us to live around people who value success, and our lives grow collectively like a snowball rolling down a ski hill.

So I hope that you practice the fundamentals contained in this book, become experts at achieving each of your goals, and then pass the passion on to those you care about.

Please remember the only true success is helping another human being in his or her journey through life.

ABOUT THE AUTHOR

GARY LANDREMAN HAS been in sales and sales management for nearly three decades. He has received numerous national awards for sales achievement and sales management accomplishments.

Gary has developed curriculum and taught sales and sales management courses to thousands throughout the United States. His unique style and approach to goal setting, planning, prospecting, time management, proper questioning, team building, training, coaching, handling objections, time management, and collecting techniques have made Gary's knowledge and training methods invaluable in the sales profession. His direct and specific methods will allow any serious person in the sales profession to instantly implement his techniques and help them increase their paychecks and become a Professional Sales Person.

Printed in the United States
77628LV00002BA/16